# LET'S TALK
# MONEY

## Praise for the earlier editions of *Let's Talk Money*

'When we think of a book on money and its management, we think of pie charts and bar charts. We think of boring, jargon-filled text. *Let's Talk Money* tries to smash all these notions and brings the reader a book that is a slice of their lives.'

*Mint Lounge*

'A one-stop read for understanding the world of personal finance. Written from the Indian household perspective, the book highlights dos and don'ts of the game.'

*Outlook Money*

'Unlike other popular books which deal with the same subject, this book has been prepared keeping the realities of the Indian society in mind.'

*Unique Times, Kochi*

'Simple does it. Peppered with anecdotes, Monika Halan's book offers easy tips on personal finance.'

*The Week*

'Not a get-rich-quick guide, this book helps you build a smart system to live your dream life rather than stay worried about the "right" investment or "perfect" insurance.'

*Financial Express 'On the Shelf'*

'Halan's toolbox is full of reader-friendly equipment. Her English is a kind of Indian English, with its exuberant syntax and commingling of other languages, which is also the language of her target audience. The writer draws on her experiences and those of her friends to whip up engaging anecdotes, homilies, similes, among others, which enliven and humanize her subject. Her engaging voice is just what a book of advice needs. Her tone is that of a friend – forthright and compassionate.'

*Moneycontrol.com*

'*Let's Talk Money* transformed the way I looked at my personal savings and I have recommended it to so many friends and colleagues. It is a must-read for youngsters who are starting their savings journey. Simple to read and easy to understand, the book is pure common sense. It should be a compulsory textbook in colleges to take forward the journey of financial literacy in our country.'
**Ashwani Bhatia, managing director, State Bank of India**

'At Banasthali Vidyapith, the world's largest residential university for women, while we were introducing the course on personal finance for the students in law and management, our board of studies recommended that *Let's Talk Money* is the best reference book and therefore we have adopted it as a core textbook. The feedback from students and teachers about this book has been excellent. It is comprehensive and adopts innovative approaches in the explanations.'
**Prof. Harsh Purohit, dean, FMS-WISDOM and Faculty of Law, Banasthali Vidyapeeth**

'Savings and investments are two different things. People who know how to save sometimes do not know how to invest, why to invest, where to invest, etc. Monika Halan has been a sane voice in Indian investment publication for over two decades. She has been a very popular and respected columnist for her views on investments which a common man can understand. I recommend all to read this book.'
**Ashish Chauhan, MD and CEO, Bombay Stock Exchange**

'Monika talks "money" to the readers in a language that is simple and easy to understand. The book focuses on the essential ways to understand what money does for us and what we need to do to ensure a balance between present needs and future security. A must-read for the young and old alike.'
**C.B. Bhave, chairman, Indian Institute for Human Settlements, and former chairman, SEBI**

'Conversational in style, and comprehensive in content, Monika Halan's *Let's Talk Money* is just what the doctor ordered. Managing one's money need not be a nightmare, even in a world where product-pushers, planners and, on occasion, regulatory action ensure that you and your money are soon parted. This should be on the top of any must-read list.'

> M. Damodaran, chairman, Excellence Enablers, and former chairman, SEBI, UTI and IDBI

'In the world of personal finance, Monika Halan stands out as a voice of enormous knowledge combined with integrity. If you wish to manage your money well and become wealthy, this book is a must-read for you.'

> Vivek Law, founder, CEO & editor-in-chief, The MoneyMile

'It's an excellent read – riding on the author's characteristic candour and domain expertise that equips her to explain financial concepts and instruments in the simplest manner without talking down to her audience.'

> Menaka Doshi, Bloomberg Quint

'Too many smart people have been led to believe that "finance is not for me". In this straight-talking book about taking control of your finances, Monika Halan addresses all the questions you've had but never asked for fear of sounding silly. Engagingly written with personal reflections, this book cuts through the clutter of products and marketing spiels to outline a system to manage money that is action-oriented and will break your stupor. A must-read for people looking to get started in their personal finance and investment journeys. Monika understands the Indian investor psyche like few others.'

> Bindu Ananth, chair, Dvara Trust

# MONIKA HALAN

# LET'S TALK MONEY

*You've Worked Hard for It,
Now Make It Work for You*

HARPER
BUSINESS

*An Imprint of* HarperCollins *Publishers*

First published in paperback in India by Harper Business 2018
An imprint of HarperCollins *Publishers*
4th Floor, Tower A, Building No. 10, DLF Cyber City,
DLF Phase II, Gurugram, Haryana – 122002
www.harpercollins.co.in

Published in hardback by Harper Business 2023
This edition published in hardback by Harper Business 2024

2 4 6 8 10 9 7 5 3 1

Copyright © Monika Halan 2018, 2021, 2023, 2024

P-ISBN: 978-93-6569-165-8
E-ISBN: 978-93-5277-940-6

The views and opinions expressed in this book are the author's own and the facts are as reported by her, and the publishers are not in any way liable for the same.

None of the content in this book is intended to be a substitute for professional financial advice and should not be relied on as financial advice. Always seek the guidance of your financial advisor with any questions you may have regarding your finances.

Monika Halan asserts the moral right
to be identified as the author of this work.

All rights reserved. No part of this publication may be reproduced, stored in a retrieval system, or transmitted, in any form or by any means, electronic, mechanical, photocopying, recording or otherwise, without the prior permission of the publishers.

Typeset in 13/17 Requiem at
Manipal Technologies, Manipal

Printed and bound at
Replika Press Pvt. Ltd.

This book is produced from independently certified FSC® paper to ensure responsible forest management.

*To the Indian income tax payer.
You pull hard for those that don't.*

**Also by Monika Halan**

*Let's Talk Mutual Funds: A Systematic,
Smart Way to Make Them Work for You* (2023)
*Let's Talk Legacy: A Financial Planner for Your Loved Ones* (2024)

# CONTENTS

|  |  |  |
|---|---|---|
|  | FOREWORD | xi |
|  | PREFACE TO THE THIRD EDITION | xvii |
|  | PREFACE TO THE SECOND EDITION | xix |
| 1. | THE MONEY ORDER | 1 |
| 2. | DON'T STASH THAT CASH! | 5 |
| 3. | EMERGENCIES NEED A FUND | 15 |
| 4. | BUILDING YOUR PROTECTION | 24 |
| 5. | WHAT IF YOU DIE? | 44 |
| 6. | FINALLY, WE'RE INVESTING | 65 |
| 7. | LET'S DE-JARGON INVESTING | 80 |
| 8. | EQUITY | 95 |
| 9. | MUTUAL FUNDS | 116 |
| 10. | PUTTING IT ALL TOGETHER | 151 |
| 11. | MY RETIREMENT | 176 |
| 12. | REDO THE BOX | 189 |
| 13. | WILL IT | 196 |
| 14. | WHAT KILLS A MONEY BOX? | 206 |
|  | WORKSHEETS | 215 |
|  | APPENDIX | 249 |
|  | LAST NOTE | 256 |
|  | ACKNOWLEDGEMENTS | 261 |
|  | INDEX | 265 |

# FOREWORD

If you're reading this book, it is because at some point, you have worried, or are currently worried, about money. Talking about money, even if you have it, is a curious taboo. We rarely have open and honest conversations about our spending and saving habits.

People may boast about great investments, like the stock that made them super-sized returns, but shy away from mentioning the strain on their financial life caused by their expensive spending habits – like that fancy coffee they order twice a day. We worry about investment the way we worry about our weight. Instead of dieting or investing being a habit, we only think of them as remedial measures when our weight or our bank balance goes too high or too low.

This is further exacerbated by the fact that the commission-driven world of finance has been deliberately obfuscated for the layman. Navigating through the jargon can feel like trying to cut through a dense thicket with a butter knife. No wonder then, like the proverbial ostrich, many of us stick our heads in the sand, hoping if we don't see the problem, it doesn't see us too. Which is why I appreciate Monika's new book. It wants us to start having honest conversations about money. This means admitting that our excuses are just that: excuses. Managing your finances is not a luxury for the rich, it is hygiene for everyone.

I know Monika from her role as consulting editor at *Mint*. In our interactions, I was always struck by her focus on the consumer. She would ask all the hard questions about complex economic affairs and then work to communicate them simply to her audience. As you reach Chapter 6 you will learn why.

Monika is not some prodigious financial genius, picking blockbuster investments since she was sixteen. In the true spirit of talking honestly about money, she humbly admits she started investing quite late, and also found it difficult to meet her saving goals in her early years. Her style of advice is not to talk down to people struggling with money, but to empower them to believe that if she did it, they can do it too.

Hence, *Let's Talk Money* is not a get-rich-quick scheme. Nor is it trying to sell you something. Unlike intermediaries who need to make themselves indispensable, Monika tries hard to make herself unnecessary after you've read the book. She doesn't just give you academic reasons for her advice, but also helpful analogies and relatable stories to explain why you should manage your finances in the way she prescribes. Her chapter on equity is full of delightful analogies that turn the intimidating task of portfolio selection into a much simpler task of choosing the right kind of vehicle for your needs. These examples are funny, but also revealing.

The value of this book, then, is not in the technical details themselves. Monika summarizes them in less than half a page in every chapter. The delight is in reading her personal stories, and those of her friends, to understand these concepts, instead of glossing over them next time someone starts talking about fixed-income products or equity-linked savings schemes. The other reason why I'm excited by the launch of *Let's Talk Money* is its timing.

If you're an investor, young or old, there is no better time for you to pick up this book than right now. India is in the middle of a digital transformation. Like I said in 2015, we are going through the WhatsApp moment of banking. What does that mean?

Today you can open a bank account in less than a minute. With eKYC, it is not just some fancy new-age banks that let you open accounts instantly, but also the nationalized banks you have come to know and trust. Monika recommends three different bank accounts: Income, Spend-It and Invest-It.

Today, that's a total of three minutes, versus three trips to the bank earlier. You need one OTP (one-time password) instead of three sets of addresses and ID proofs, along with some thirty-odd signatures. Moreover, you can access all of these bank accounts from any one app using UPI (unified payment interface). No need to worry about updating three passbooks every month.

The app you choose doesn't even have to be your own bank's app; interoperability means that you can choose the one that suits you the best. Mutual funds, once thought to be the investment instrument of the elite only, are now available, starting in sachets less than Rs 500 a month. Even gold is being sold digitally!

Technology like IndiaStack has reduced the friction between intent and action to almost zero. It has also meant the removal of unnecessary intermediaries whose commissions are not in line with your needs. Many of the principles in this book can be set up once and forgotten, thanks to where we are today in terms of technology. You can start investing in a completely paperless, presence-less and cashless manner.

But reducing friction is a trick for savings. Technology can also help you nudge your behaviour by increasing friction for areas of spending. There could be apps that ask you to enter two OTPs for that unnecessary e-commerce purchase. Instead of the classic 'upsize', new-age food-ordering apps could prompt you to maybe 'downsize' the fries, saving your health and your money.

Further innovations, like the recently announced account aggregators, will give you a consolidated view of all your finances, helping you track, analyse and better decide how to implement the plan that Monika will shortly arm you with. Especially if you're a first-time investor – it is a truly exciting time. The sophisticated yet simple-to-use tools available to digital-native investors were never available to us of an earlier generation.

I hope you will enjoy this book and, by the end of it, can talk money both honestly and confidently. By picking up this book you've already taken a great first step. Let me not stand in the way of you and your riches.

Nandan Nilekani<br>
2018

# PREFACE TO THE THIRD EDITION

You hold in your hands the third edition of the book that has been read, implemented, loved and gifted over and over again. More than 1,00,000 copies have been sold till date.

A third edition! If you are wondering why, then I must tell you the three good reasons to update *Let's Talk Money* in 2024, just six years after its publication.

One, the pace of change of the financial sector is so fast that there is a need to update some of the facts and figures. It is not just the regulation that changes, but also the behaviour of the industry. Then there are tax changes almost every year that make a difference to investment choices. For example, taxation of debt funds got a major setback in Budget 2023, impacting your money; therefore, revisions to the earlier editions of the book.

Then, as I updated the expense ratios, I realized that these have crept up for some debt fund categories and come down for some equity fund categories. This is interesting because till just a few years back, the debt funds – being more institutional in their demand – had expense ratios much lower than their expense-ratio ceiling limits and equity funds being mostly retail, had expense ratios near their ceiling limits. As I updated the numbers, I found that this had changed. A mix of regulatory action and competition has shaved off many basis points off many equity-funds expense ratios.

Two, I have added a sheaf of worksheets in this edition to make the chapters easier to put into action. You can create your own cash flow, emergency funds and life insurance worksheets using the templates given. I have also used two tables – compounding table and annual savings factor table – to give you tools to calculate the future values of goals and what they translate to in terms of per-year savings. Many of you cannot use Excel sheets to do this math and I hope you will spend some time to get familiar and use them to your advantage. You will use these two tables extensively to work out your short-, medium- and long-term goals and your retirement goals and savings targets.

Three, each chapter now has a couple of illustrations that try and give the main learnings in an easy-to-understand visual aid.

As you begin this journey I leave you with one thought: Each time you have a good money outcome, I feel that I have won. This feeling is literally more than money for me! So, continue to share your stories at mailme@monikahalan.com

Wishing you a rich money journey ahead.

# PREFACE TO THE SECOND EDITION

## Your money oxygen mask in times of uncertainty

*Nothing prepared us for the Covid-19 pandemic. A global crisis of this scale that threatens both life, health, income and wealth at the same time was never built into any planning calculation. The lessons from Covid-19 are important for both our lives and our money.*

In all the calculations of a disaster, financial planners had perhaps never thought of building in scenarios of the whole world stalling at the same time. Covid-19 has been that event which has seen planners and advisors rushing to the drawing board to rewrite some protocols. What can you do when there are no safe havens, when your very existence – both through health and wealth – is in trouble. It is like something out of an end-of-the-world movie that has come true.

I must admit that I have rethought 'conservative' myself due to the pandemic. Since I understand the markets and mutual funds, I have had a 90 per cent allocation to equity in my portfolio. Both my husband and I rethought our own allocation, owing to the fact that there are less years ahead of us than a younger person, both in terms of health and income. A job loss in our prime earning years would hit very badly. And it is not the market crack of 30 per cent in March 2020 that triggered this rethink – because both of us have done the math to show us that markets go up and down and this crack will finally fill, as have the others before this time. We redid our math and have settled on a 30:70 debt-equity ratio as our target. Without selling a single unit of an equity fund, we began securing our zero-risk money in a fixed deposit that would allow us to ride out two years of expenses, the rest is incremental investments into debt funds till we reach our target allocation. When the information changes, it is smart to change your mind.

The lockdown showed our own spending, investing, eating and exercising habits clearly. It has been a mirror that was covered and now is reflecting everything clearly. It showed us that working from home is a viable option. Not traveling is an option. Looking after nutrition and health are possible.

## What the pandemic taught us about our money

The first lesson I learnt is that we spend more than we need to. When the first credit card bill came that reflected the time under lockdown, I thought there was a mistake. I consider myself a frugal spender, only spending on things I want rather than random purchases made on a whim, but even my bill was down to 10 per cent of earlier spends. Going out of the house for work means higher expenses on petrol, clothes, footwear, bags, coffee, eating out, entertainment and so on. The lockdown also prevented anything other than basics to get delivered by e-commerce firms, so out went any other purchases. Most of the salaried workers saw reduced salaries, but despite the lower take-home, our savings went up. Other than EMIs, rent, domestic-helper salaries and basics, the expenses crashed. The experience of living on so little in a month is a powerful lesson to those who have always said with a self-deprecating shake of the head: I have no money to save! All those people who complained of too much month at the end of the money now find too much money at the end of the month. *My learning was that I can up my saving target sharply the day I decide to go back into a lockdown mode even once we are out of this situation.*

The second lesson I learnt was that the emergency fund amount needs to be recalibrated according to the age, stage and nature of work. I have maintained a six-month emergency fund kitty knowing that both our jobs are fairly secure, even though we are in high-risk private sector contract jobs. But as we entered the lockdown and the fact that no job is secure (other than those who work with the government with secure jobs and benefits), we found that age was not on our side and decided to ramp up our emergency fund to two years' expenses in a fixed deposit. I have never been a fan of FDs simply because of the more efficient options of debt funds available. But thinking through end-of-the-world scenarios and living through them are two different things. The need for zero-risk money needed for survival in a safe bank (PSU or one of the large private sector banks) suddenly become manifest. *My recommendation of emergency funds has now changed. For those forty years and below in secure jobs, you are fine with six months of living expenses in an FD, but as the age increases and as the riskiness of the job goes up, ramp up the fund to reach two years for older cohorts in jobs that are not that secure.*

The third lesson was that we need to rethink risk. First half of 2020 saw a private sector bank freeze deposits for a few days. During those days it was not that clear what the final outcome would be. It saw a huge market crash. It saw a fund house shut down six debt funds, freezing investor money for the near future. It saw salaries go down. It saw jobs at risk. It saw firings. Nothing felt safe. And in this panic came the lesson that there is no financial product without risk. It is just the kind of risk that is different. You can keep cash under your mattress, but what if the notes get demonetized. You can keep your money in a bank, but what if the bank fails (though in India, a scheduled commercial bank has never failed depositors, only investors into bank shares and bonds have lost money, never the depositors). You can invest in debt funds, but they can be shut down or see losses due to the kind of bonds held or due to the lack of a market to sell the holdings of the bonds in. You can invest in equity, but it can suddenly shave your wealth by half. Gold is great, but capital losses happen in this investment as well. *The fact is that there is no one safe haven for your money. Each investment comes with some risk and you have to decide which one you are able to take.* A good way to deal with this question is answered in the next point.

And this brings me to the fourth lesson – *asset allocation is not an option, and even high-risk appetite people like me need to be less risk-happy.* And those with very little risk appetite need to go for a more balanced portfolio. We need to understand the difference between risk appetite and risk capacity. Risk capacity is the ability to take risk. Risk appetite is the willingness to take risk. Capacity is about your age, stage, number of dependents, confidence about your ability to keep generating income for a long time. A younger person will have more capacity to take risk than an older person. A person with fewer dependents will have more capacity to take risk than a person with many dependents. Appetite is the desire to take risk. This depends on how well you understand money, finance, your own skills, your own ability to manage your portfolio or ability to hire a planner to do this work. My biggest lesson was that both risk capacity and appetite need to be aligned. I have a large appetite for risk because I have done the math on how markets work and what a recovery period of a crash looks like. But my capacity due to age and being in a high-risk profession is low. Ideally my own asset allocation needs to have at least 30 per cent debt. My lesson during this pandemic was to raise my allocation to debt from here on. My strategy is not to sell equity, but to put incremental flows into debt, after securing two years of living costs in an FD.

A fifth lesson was to keep debts from being too large to service. Those born after the turn of the century have a very different relationship with debt than people born earlier. Both households and firms who were not leveraged, or not under too much of a debt burden, have a greater capacity to ride a crisis. *Ideally your total fixed obligation-to-income ratio (FOIR) should be 30 per cent or less.* This means that all your EMIs put together must not be more than 30 per cent of your take home money. If your take-home is Rs 1 lakh, your EMIs are no larger than Rs 30,000. Remember, this is a maximum. I would be much happier with a 15–20 per cent ratio. Imagine a salary cut of 25 per cent and then look at your paying capacity. Keep it conservative when taking loans. Paying minimum balance on credit cards, revolving balances on cards and taking money from online lenders are all borrowing behaviour that will cause a crisis in case of reduced salary or a job loss. The closer you get to retirement age, the lesser loan burden you should carry because at retirement you need to be zero debt.

**What it taught us about our life**

Nikhil called up really worried. He has been a close family friend for decades and being younger than us, tends to take his role as a protector seriously and worries about our well-being constantly. The pandemic fears really got to him and looking at the cascading cases in Delhi in June 2020, he wanted to move some 30 people close to him to a secure location with no contact with the outside world. His point was that we should not look back at this time and say: we should have moved. I look at risk differently. And in the conversation that followed, it emerged that his real worry was for his minor children. The way we behave when we have dependents is very different than when we don't. With our only child financially self-sufficient, both my husband's and my fears of death are limited. We have our wills ready and also have the faith that when the time comes, the good friend Yama will come and find us wherever we are. Of course, this does not mean irresponsible behaviour of not sanitizing, not wearing masks or not maintaining social distancing. I wrote about this before, but here goes again – we have to decide how much protection we need. Go out wearing a seat belt in a fully serviced car with tested breaks and good tyres or go out in an armoured car, fearing an accident? We need to choose the protection we want.

My learning from the crisis was also about living each day as if it is one of the last few. This is a crisis that can touch your nose with its greedy finger and say tag, you're it, however much you try and avoid it. This is a good time to make your own peace with your own death. We believe we are immortal and live as if there is no end to either youth or life. Making peace with death is about looking after those you love after you are gone, especially when you have underage kids. Write down what your aspirations are for the kids. Identify a group of three friends and relatives who you trust fully and who will have the best interest of your kids if you and spouse are gone. Three is a good number and prevents a change of heart of any one person who is in a sole position of decision making. This is a good time to revisit the chapters on life insurance and wills. Making peace with your own death or that of your loved ones is also very empowering and liberating. It encourages you to be independent, it encourages you to exit toxic relationships and it makes small trivial irritants of living with other human beings just that – small and trivial. This is actually a great lesson to learn – how to live each day as if it were one of the last few, but also how to live each day as if it was just another of thousands ahead. That balance if you can find, is the balance of life! And Nikhil is now working on a will that looks after the interests of his dependents and has given up the idea of leaving town.

## Learnings about work

A very important career learning also emerged from the pandemic and the hit that incomes, which jobs and enterprise took in the private sector. We all need a Plan B and a Plan C. The pandemic showed the ugly side of some workplaces with bosses turning into bullies who would blackmail staff into working without a break, 12-hour days, 5 days a week. The weekend too was fair game for work calls, mails, meetings and deadlines. A friend shared that she would take the phone to the loo, so afraid she was of missing the boss' calls and then getting an earful for not picking up the phone. There were skipped meals because you could not leave your workstation for 10 minutes without getting calls, messages and pings from the boss's personal staff. This is a toxic workplace and such places need to be exited. At every age and stage, other than the emergency fund that is also the money you need to quit a toxic workplace, you need a strategy to be always employable. The pandemic has come at a time when a shift is on in the workplace. Just as computers and automation made some jobs redundant 30 years ago, robotics, artificial intelligence and technology is getting ready to take the world to the next level of work. Everyone needs to do two things. One, don't fall into routine work. Always strive for a deeper understanding of what you do and then try and stretch beyond what the ask is. I remember telling all the new reporters who would come to work with me – there are no boring beats (jargon for areas of reporting – for example, finance ministry is a 'beat' or 'crime' is a beat), only boring journalists. It is up to you to bring attention, intelligence and creativity in the most mundane and boring of jobs. Two, you need to plan for a career 10 years ahead of today. What would you want to be doing 10 years from today and what are you going to do about it today. Have a second and a third career cooking on the slow fire even as you raise the flame to max on your current work. Think of the work you do and not the job you have. You may not have a job, but you can always have work. So, look at what value you bring to the table and sharpen your own value proposition.

There are two cohorts worst hit by a crisis like the pandemic. Those entering the job market and those close to exiting it. The cohort that came into the job market just after the 2008 North Atlantic Financial Crisis saw a tight job market. Friends from that cohort have shared that it took MBAs from ace institutes almost a decade to recover from the entry-level reduced salary to match what other cohorts were earning. One option for such a situation is to take a gap year and do something that adds to the resume, so that by the time you return to the job market, hopefully it has recovered. Not everybody has this luxury of taking a year out and must get down to competing for the few jobs at reduced entry-level salaries than are offered in a bull market and economy phase. The advantage this cohort has is of age and of a long runway ahead to recover from this initial hit on job opportunities. The pre-retirement cohort in their 50s is almost the worst hit by a calamity like this. In a column I wrote for *Mint*, I called this cohort 'ageing, entrenched and expensive'. When a firm is cost-cutting hysterically to deal with both a demand and a supply shock, the deadwood gets cleaned out. Each worker has to justify her place in the firm. The cohort in their 50s is the most expensive having seen 30 years of increments and salary rises. They are also usually reluctant to adopt new technologies and change. Getting fired in the highest earning years of your life reduces the runway for your retirement corpus targeting. This is the decade in which a bulk of retirement savings happen since the kids are usually financial independent. The job loss at this age also means that the chances of another parallel job are very low. This cohort needs to tank up on own medical insurance, get ready with its retirement corpus quickly by cutting down on spends and also reducing goals of kids' education and marriage if these are not behind you already. This cohort needs to put on their oxygen masks first.

I wrote this when we were in the middle of the pandemic in India – June 2020. Literally at this point, we don't know what is ahead. But I know that there are things which happen for which no amount of prior planning is good enough. We read about such events in stories. We watch movies about rags to riches and riches to rags due to events out of our control. And if all that we have planned for fails, well then, there is no option but dust off the crisis once it passes, get back on your feet and find the best options possible to rekindle the life you lived.

Uncertainty got a new name with Covid-19 for our health, life, income and wealth. While the basic principles remain the same, there are some lessons learnt from this crisis for our health and our wealth.

**You are doing okay if**

1. you have between six months to two years of emergency funds in a mix of FD in a scheduled commercial large bank – both public sector and private sector banks are fine – and very conservative debt funds;
2. your loans are less than 30 per cent of your take-home salary;
3. you are increasing safe assets as you age;
4. you have your own medical cover;
5. you have your wills in place; and
6. you are building a second and a third career even as you work your current job.

# 1

# THE MONEY ORDER

*Our money worries usually centre around finding the best return on investment. But there is a lot more to financial fitness than just investments. We need a system and not a single-shot solution.*

We feel guilty about the mess in our money lives. Almost like a sound playing constantly in the background that becomes louder in moments of silence, a cold dread that lingers just at the back of everyday life. We worry about not doing enough, about not making the 'smart' decisions, about missing the moneymaking train as it zips past, about not having enough for our kids and ourselves in future years.

We worry about ageing parents and their long-term care. But most of all, we worry about emergencies and hoard cash. The cash accumulates, and then some sharpshooter comes along and offers this fantastic deal. He's persistent; pushy; throws numbers; works on your fears, emotions, guilt. And gets your money. This ends in several ways. In a total loss, a partial loss or simply a bad investment that gives you returns worse than a bank FD (fixed deposit).

This book is a conversation about money. At the end of reading it, you will be able to organize your finances in a manner that allows you to get on with your life, with all its complications, rather than stay worried about the 'right' investment. We'll build a system rather than a single-shot solution.

Think of your financial life as a money box. The money box fills in your working–earning years with income; you use the money to pay for living costs, fees, rent, EMIs (equated monthly instalments), taxes, insurances and vacations, and a whole long list of what it takes to live the Indian urban mass affluent life. Usually the box shows a surplus left behind at the bottom each month.

This gets invested for future use. Along the way you dip into your money box to pay for your kids' higher education, their marriages, and then finally when you get too old to earn (we all get there – just look at your grandparents or parents), the box begins to fill with pensions and other investment income like interest, dividend and profit.

The mistake most people make, and we are not to blame, is to think of the money box only as a container of investment products. We start thinking about what to invest in – should I buy a plot of land, or should I buy shares, or should I invest in that pension plan – to solve our money worry. But 'what to invest in' is not the first decision we should take – a mistake that we all make, pushed as we are by a sales commission–

driven insurance industry or a next-new-thing–driven mutual fund industry.

So, how should we think about our money box? A good money box is one that allows you to streamline your cash flows. It builds in safety nets for preserving your savings in the face of an emergency – typically a medical emergency, a job loss, or death of a salary-earning family member.

Insurances have a purpose in a money box. We'll understand what that purpose is. No, it is not wealth creation. Product choice becomes much easier if you understand *why* you need that product in the first place. Then, finally, we come to investing and understand what suits us and how to build our portfolio.

The book is about helping you construct this box by understanding your own needs and situation. It is not a get-rich-quick book. The goal is to make you feel more confident about your money life, but in a system that allows you to be hands-free for most of the year, needing to open the box no more than twice a year.

The by-product of this exercise is that you will actually be able to fund all the things and save for goals that are important to you. This is not easy work and your unique money box will take six months to construct. But once done, you have a grid that works on its own and needs a minor tweak just once in a while.

Interwoven into this book are stories and case studies of some of the hundreds of people who have written to me on the four TV shows I have done, in the past, and responded to the column I wrote in *Mint*. Equally interwoven is a larger perspective of why we are faced with a marketplace that is predatory. You will understand why the government's need to finance its deficit leads to you buying toxic products.

Yup, there's a link. You will understand why the global financial sector wants you to feel stupid. You will understand how you are actually doing the best you can in a marketplace that is full of sharks. You will see that you are not a money dummy.

Think about it: How does the toughest value-for-money kitna-deti-hai person suddenly become stupid when it comes to money?

You will understand that the current 'buyer beware' in the financial sector – or transferring of responsibility to the investor of buying the right financial product – is a regulatory failure. It is not unlike a car vendor flinging open the bonnet and saying: 'Go do your due diligence and ensure this car is safe.'

Asking an average person to understand concepts of present value, future value, real return and so on is no different from asking him to buy a car after ensuring that the engine is safe! You will understand why the regulatory changes under way are so important for your future.

The book is not going to give you a prescriptive road map. It is more of a direction. A way to think about your financial life with some rules of thumb that you can modify according to your own situation. You need to engage with it and personalize it.

May your money box be full of good things, always.

## 2

# DON'T STASH THAT CASH!

*Most financial planning fails because we don't have an efficient cash-flow system in place. The chapter tells you how to build your own system of managing inflows and outflows each month.*

Anupama Gajwani is not the usual Indian woman you run into. Growing up with an artist dad in a house filled with paintings and the smell of turpentine, my childhood friend Anu and I are as different as it comes.

My steady, boring, planned ant-like world contrasts with her 'let's-eat-that-goddam-lemon-tart-now!' life. A freelance designer, Anu is a single mom and lives from assignment to assignment, and thinks nothing of taking off to Toronto to see her son cleaning out her bank account.

I've never bothered to talk money with her because planning is not what she does, and it sounds boring when you have so many cool stories to hear! It must be age, or stage, or a bolt from the sky above that got her; but early January last year when we met for one of our Sunday lunch sessions, her new passion was getting her money life in order.

'Hey! Hey! Hey! You have to help me. I will do this. Now. Now. Now!' Not your usual mid-forties person for sure. 'I have no idea where my money goes. I know when it comes into the bank, but after that it is a blur,' she says.

Not knowing where our money goes is not a problem peculiar to a certain personality. Think back: Don't you remember saying, 'I have no idea where my money goes?' Or, 'I have nothing left to save.' Or the worst one: 'What investing plan – where is the money?'

One of the key reasons we make these statements is that we don't have an effective cash-flow system. Everybody has money to save – from the poor woman who sells veggies to you on the roadside, to the tycoon driving by in his Bimmer – we just don't know how to look for it.

The key to finding the money to save and invest is to have a good cash-flow system. Sounds like what a company does or the kirana store owner needs to do, and not a salaried professional, right?

Think of a cash-flow system as simply a way to demarcate your money between spending and saving. Chances are that you do have a system in place but it is rough and not well-defined. Your system keeps your income and expenditure largely in sync, but you've not given it a defined form.

Money drops in each month and the living costs kick in immediately: rent or EMI gets debited; domestic help salaries get paid; utility bills are done; groceries are bought; fees are paid; travel costs are an ongoing daily expenditure as are lifestyle costs – shopping, gadgets, eating out, movies. The rest of the money goes off to pay the credit card bill, inflated from indulging in the end-of-season sale last month.

I know that a lot of the money conversation begins with efficient budgeting. We are told to write down every rupee we spend. To be meticulous about it. But I find that boring …

milk    –  Rs    150
eggs    –  Rs    100
petrol  –  Rs    2,500
coffee  –  Rs    100
lunch   –  Rs    600 …

Then tomorrow, the same exercise. And then again. Two things happen if you track each expense down meticulously. One, you get bored and junk the whole exercise after a week of being good. Two, you get obsessive about money and forget to enjoy the coffee or the dinner, as you busily think about how much you've spent today.

If you have a good way to budget and need the discipline, go ahead and use one of the many apps to track your spending, but if you find that tough to do, just work with the cash-flow system.

The goal of the cash-flow system in the money-box world is to conceive of the least troublesome method of managing inflows and outflows of money, and doing it in a manner that automatically separates spending from saving money.

I don't know about you, but I have had this experience many times over: Whatever may be the amount of cash in the wallet or in the home cash box, it gets spent. Large chunks of unused money cry out to be used, and get borrowed away or spent on an impulse that later you wonder why you gave into.

I remember once being talked into lending a large sum of money to a friend (no longer a friend) for a non-emergency situation. She couldn't manage her expenses and needed help. I bought into the sob story and moved the money. When better sense prevailed, the cash was already gone. It took me more than two years of nagging to get it back. Not a nice place to be in – you lose the money, and you lose respect for the other person, and somewhere for yourself, for getting into a situation like this. That was a lesson well learnt. I move the money away from temptation. I found a useful way of doing that.

I'll tell you about an easy cash-flow system that I use. And then I'll tell you the science behind it. The goal is to separate out money according to its function so that the brain is better able to map it. I do this using three boxes for the three functions of money. These are income, spending and saving. If we can separate the money into these three boxes each month, we'll be in better control.

To do this is harder than you'd think. I use three bank accounts. I give them names. Giving names is very important. For those of us who eat meat, would we be able to eat a chicken that had a name?

Suppose there was Cheeku the chicken running around the front lawn – would we be able to eat him? Don't think so. A name gives something an identity and we hate to violate that identity. So I give names to the three accounts. My salary account I label 'Income Account'. The second account I call 'Spend-It Account'. The third is called 'Invest-It Account'.

Once your salary hits your Income Account, within thirty minutes (OK, take a day – but do it) move out your monthly expenditure to your Spend-It Account. And whatever is left, move it to your Invest-It Account. Salary accounts are usually zero-balance accounts, so sweeping all the money out is possible. But if you like to leave little pockets of cash for that little bit extra spending, like I do, keep a few thousands in your Income Account as a cash reserve.

I remember one relationship manager of my salary account calling me very upset at the money moving out so fast. Why's he upset – because the longer the money stays in the bank, the better he manages to meet his deposit target, or the target of getting a certain amount of deposits in the bank each month.

Why does the bank want higher deposits? Because your money is lent out to others – loans earn the bank anywhere between 10 per cent to 18 per cent, while you get around 2.7 to 4.25 per cent interest on your savings deposit. The difference between what you get and what the bank earns, minus costs, is the bank's profit.

Getting back to our accounts. Use your Income Account as the sump for all kinds of money inflow that we get. You may quickly say: 'Oh, but I get only a salary.' But there is always some other cash that flows into your life. Cash gifted by parents or relatives, a bonus, a refund from work, a matured insurance plan, rent from a property you own, dividend on stocks or mutual funds, return of money borrowed. Other than interest earned in the other two accounts, rest of the inflow into your life falls into one account – your Income Account.

Next, remove from the Income Account the money you spend each month. We all roughly know what the monthly expenditure flow is like – we know that we spend 25,000 or 40,000, or a lakh (100,000) or more on living costs. Give yourself a little spending cushion in the first few months of creating this system and move 10–15 per cent more than what you think you spend into your Spend-It Account. That's all you have for this month's expenses – rent, EMI, food, salaries to pay, fuel, credit card bills, utilities, pocket money, medicines, whatever.

Set a calendar alert if the month ahead has a premium payment due for a medical, house, car or term plan, and move that much more money to take care of this additional spend.

Now, whatever is left in your Income Account, move it, in another thirty seconds (OK, at most thirty minutes!), to your Invest-It Account. For this system to work, you need to be using online banking and online investing tools. Getting your money online is a key to hands-free money management. Spend some time getting the online life right, so that when it is done, the system is smooth and friction-free.

Remember what the goal is: to have a hands-free money life. Remember what we're doing right now is about creating a system so that, once it is in place, you can execute your monthly money moves in thirty seconds.

When I began doing this, it took me a long time to streamline my financial life so that it fell into these neat boxes. We have joint accounts with all kinds of family members, and getting everybody to buy into your system at home is an exercise. Begin with yourself and, if your partner is not helping, create your own system first. You and your spouse must have your individual Income Accounts. The Spend-It Account is a joint account into which both credit equal amounts for the monthly spending.

Each partner has his and her Invest-It Account in different banks. These can be joint, but the primary holder should ideally be the person in whose name the investment will happen. Don't do anything else. Don't think about investing. Just get these three accounts in place. Once they are, start the exercise of moving money out on the day your salary hits the Income Account.

Remember, we're not investing yet — so the money in your Invest-It Account is just sitting there. That's fine. We have to make a plan for the next fifty to eighty years ahead — what is three months of practice? For three months, watch your own spending pattern — is the money you thought you needed enough? Too little? Too much? Whatever your situation, you'll get a grip on how much you spend each month by watching how much you move to your Spend-It Account at the beginning of the month. I'd leave a bit extra in the Income Account in the first three months to see how much I need in my Spend-It Account. If it runs dry, move more from Income to Spend-It. *Moving money from Invest-It to Spend-It is not allowed in my book.*

In three months you'll know what's going on with your money life. If your Invest-It Account is empty, you know you're spending too much. You should be able to move a minimum of 10 per cent of your income in hand each month to your Invest-It Account – irrespective of EMI, rent and whatever else your commitments are. Sneak a peek at the retirement chapter if you are impatient to find out thumb rules on how much you need to save at each age and stage.

Two things happened when I began doing this. One, I began to question my spending. Once you realize how much is going into your Spend-It Account, you can't hide from yourself any more. Two, as the Invest-It Account begins to build up, you see how much your saving capacity is.

I've had friends WhatsApp me six months later and say, 'I never thought I could save, and look at what I have in my account now!' Putting a label of Invest-It deters most people from dipping into it for a splurge.

What stops you from dipping into your Invest-It Account to pay for your spending? This is where behavioural economics steps in. Putting a label on money prevents people from using it for any other purpose. This is called 'mental accounting' and it means that we like to separate our money into separate accounts according to intent, and dislike using it for any other use.

When we use mental accounting unconsciously we end up using it wrongly – carrying a large credit-card debt that costs us 36 per cent interest a year, while making the monthly payments to the recurring deposit that gives just 7 per cent interest.

A smarter step will be to pay off the high-cost loan before spending, but mental accounts prevent us from seeing the two uses of money with the same lens. When we use mental accounting in the cash-flow system, we are using the principle of mental accounting to work for us. When we label the account Invest-It Account, we will be loath to touch it for our current spending needs. We're tricking our brain into doing the right thing.

It's done. We've got a cash-flow system in place. We're one step forward in our journey to a hands-free money box. And yes, Anu saw the logic of the system, and is using it. And is on her way to a smart money box.

You can create your own cash-flow statement by filling the worksheet on page 215.

> Budgets are boring. Instead of mapping the small expenses, have these rules of thumb in your mind. If you are going consistently over these limits, you need a relook at where your money is going. Eating out, going to the movies, travelling and buying gadgets are the big budget breakers. Go for a balanced, rather than a hard, spending diet. Hard diets fail.
> **You are doing okay if**
>
> 1. you have a three-account system that separates your income, spending and savings;
> 2. your spending on living costs is no more than 45–50 per cent of your take-home income;
> 3. your EMI payouts are no more than 25–30 per cent of your take-home income; and
> 4. your savings are at least 15–20 per cent of your take-home income.

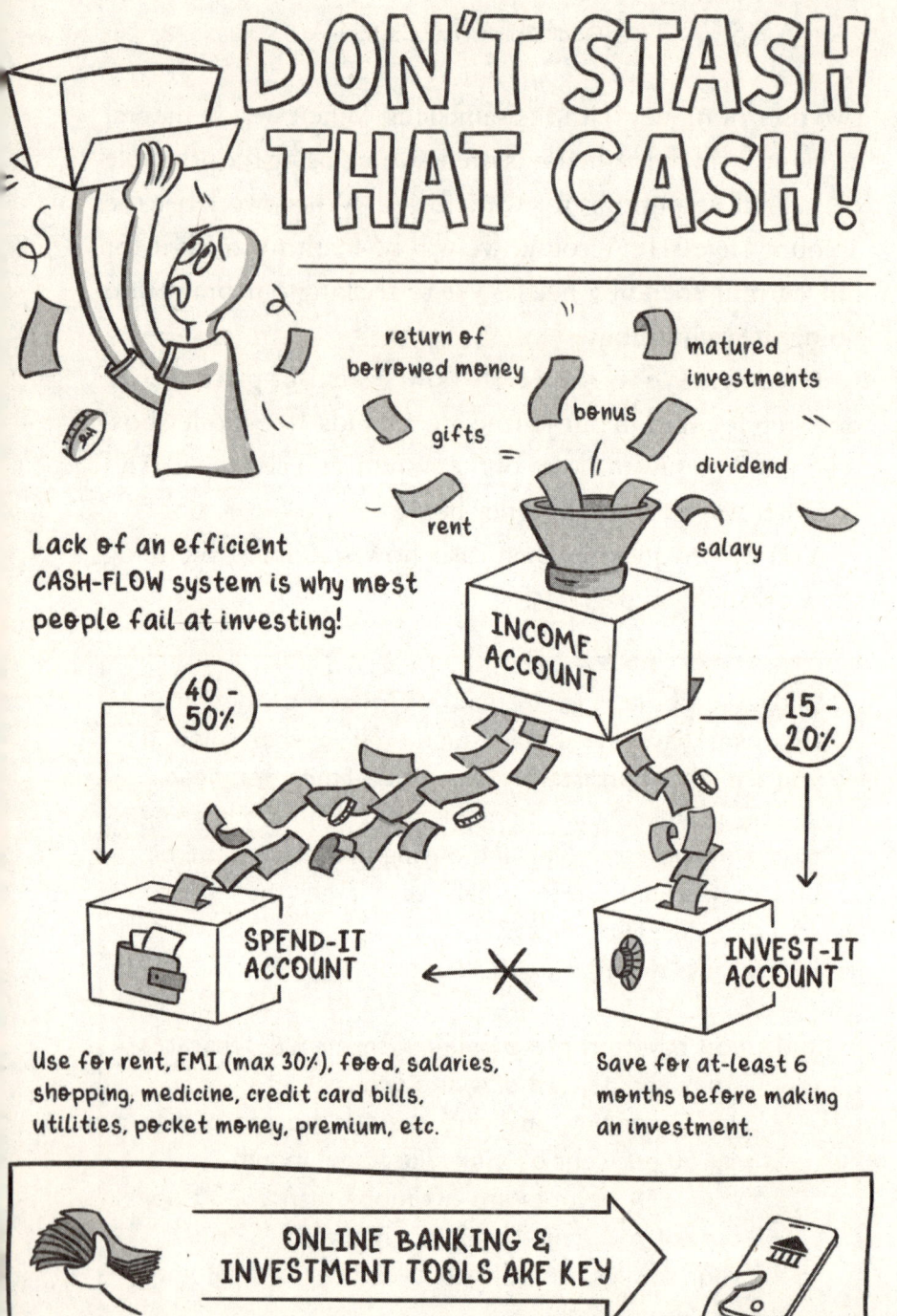

# 3

# EMERGENCIES NEED A FUND

*Keeping money ready for an emergency is important. Not only do you not have to worry about the money when you need it but it also frees up money for long-term investments.*

My daughter was just five when she understood the importance of a car seat belt. I would drive her to and back from a nearby school and insist that she belt up in the front seat or the back seat, wherever she chose to sit. Five is the age when 'why' and 'won't' are at the top of the vocabulary charts. A growing sense of self allows the knee-high two-pound tigers to assert their independence. But, this was an argument I won, since it was non-negotiable. It is not often that I use the 'I'm-bigger-and-smarter-and-you're-just-a-little-kid' line of parental control, but this was one of those times.

Anyhow. So, kid gives in with bad grace and sulks for a couple of days. Then gets used to it. One afternoon we're returning home, the usual idiot in a BMW brakes too hard in front of our car – he probably thinks he's in a commercial, showing off the dead-stop prowess of his roadrunner. I slam my brakes and we both fly forward, get restrained by the belt and miss having our heads crash through the front windshield. I exhale, call the guy some really bad names – mentally, of course, kid mustn't know mumma knows these words – and then swing back into the traffic.

Two minutes later a small voice goes – belt ne pakad liya, the belt held me back. Kid also realizes that the responsibility of staying in the seat now belonged to the belt, and it can then focus on other stuff, like consuming a steaming bhutta (corn) using both hands, rather than one.

Take a moment to reflect and tell me yourself why you are afraid of long-term money commitments. I've had hundreds of people who have called in on the various TV shows I've done, and each time I've asked the question 'Why don't you want to invest for the long-term?', the answer almost always is 'What if there is an emergency? I won't be able to use my own money if it is tied up in a long-term investment.'

The unwillingness to take risks also comes from this fear of not having the money when it is needed. Therefore, people stay with money in near-liquid products or bank deposits that are easily cashed if need arises.

It is a reasonable fear. We all do have situations where we need the money – it could be a medical emergency, a job loss, some disability or health issue that prevents us from earning.

But there is a way to keep money aside for such emergencies and then free up our savings for the future.

Let's understand the logic of having a defined emergency fund. You'd typically need money 'midway' under two circumstances – planned and unplanned events. Think about your car. You know that the car will go for servicing, and will need money for that. You know that after seven to eight years there will be costs associated with repair and possibly the cost of a new car. This stuff we can plan for. In life, the planned expenses – such as buying a car, making the down payment for a house, sending kid to biz school, going on a foreign holiday, staying fifteen days at Jindal Farms to cure your back problem, sending brother to detox in Ananda – are all things you can prepare for. We'll talk about planning for such events in Chapter 10 and what products work best for different goals.

What about the unplanned things – like the car getting rammed while quietly parked outside the house and needing a fender change? These are unplanned expenses, and unless you have a comprehensive car cover, you will be out of pocket for the cost of getting the car back in shape. There are many such unplanned emergency expenses that living our urban mass affluent life brings us: a large hospital bill, getting fired and not having an income, Chennai-like floods needing a full replacement of the basement furniture and gadgets. Or the 2020 pandemic – nobody was prepared for that, not even financial planners. It is for such reasons that we create an emergency fund and buy insurances.

There are some events that we can look after through insurances, but there are some, like a job loss, that we need to prepare for. We all need an emergency fund. This is a fund that will only be used in case of a financial emergency. We clearly label it in our heads as an emergency fund and don't tap into it. No, you can't use it even for the down payment of the house. This is the piggy bank you break only when you need the money for an unplanned emergency.

A friend and her husband were in high-paying advertising jobs. High earners also spend well and they bought their condo in Gurugram on a bank loan. The wife's income went towards the EMI fully, and the husband's ran the house and went towards savings. The wife got pregnant and there were complications. She had to quit work to have the baby. She could go back to work in 9–12 months, but for the next year there was no EMI money.

There are some choices in life you wish you did not have. Baby or house is not a decision anybody can make. Of course she quit. They scraped together all their savings, borrowed from family and prepaid a part of the loan so that the rest of the EMI could be serviced by the husband's salary. They did have to cut back on lifestyle in a big way for a couple of years. The baby came, was wonderful, and my friend went back to work in two years. But it was a hairy time in their lives.

Having an emergency fund gives you a cushion for such an event. It allows you to think clearly and not take hasty decisions, like selling the house and moving to another place – something that the couple contemplated for a while. I have personally made use of my own emergency fund on at least two occasions. Let me just say that when the time comes, you will look back at your younger self and thank her with your older self wholeheartedly!

## How much do you need?

A rough rule of thumb says keep aside six months' to two years' living costs. Include everything in it – rent, EMI, school fees, utilities, premiums, credit card charges, club memberships, whatever. The cash-flow system that we created earlier will tell you what your monthly transfer to your Spend-It Account is. Multiply that by six.

Remember this is an average; you can increase or decrease this amount depending on your personal situation. Suppose both you and your spouse earn – the probability of both of you losing jobs at the same time is low; in addition, if there are no dependents – you are a double-income no-kids household.

In such lower-risk households, the emergency fund amount can be reduced to three months' spending. But if one salary is fully going towards the EMI, it makes sense to have a bit more than six months' living costs in the emergency fund, and not less.

On the other extreme, if you are the sole earner of a house that has your spouse, kids and parents to support, along with an EMI to pay, you're better off having up to a year's worth of spending in the emergency fund. So, lower the risk to the household, lower is the number of months' spending you need to cover for in the emergency fund. And higher the risk, higher the amount you save. Specially for people in their 50s, an emergency fund of two years becomes useful when negotiating a bizarre event like the 2020 pandemic that caused salary cuts and job losses.

I'm risk-averse when it comes to my emergency fund, and I keep two years' expenses in a clearly marked emergency fund. We'll see how this allows me to take much more risk with my investments than I would otherwise. But that's in Chapter 8.

## Where do you keep this money?

We want to be able to access this money quickly with no loss in value. The worst thing you can do is leave this money sloshing around in your savings deposit. At the time of writing this book, State Bank of India gave 2.70 per cent interest on the savings deposit. You need to move it to a place that is not that easy to access, but yet is liquid enough to be of use when you want it and gives a return that is better than a savings deposit.

The easiest and best-understood product is a fixed deposit. We've all grown up with our dads going to get money 'fixed', and now we can use the new banking technology to move money into, and withdraw money from, FDs without going through the painful process of filling out the form at the branch.

This is your entry-level product – setting up an FD with

your emergency money in it. If you are banking with a bank that allows flexi-FDs that allow you to sweep out just the amount you need, rather than breaking the entire deposit, go for that. Else split your emergency fund into smaller FDs so that you don't have to lose the interest on the entire deposit.

People familiar with mutual funds can use what are called short-term debt funds to build an emergency fund. We'll talk about mutual funds in greater detail in Chapter 9, but at this stage you just need to know that mutual funds have many kinds of products and some of these are suited for needs such as an emergency fund. But if you are not familiar with funds, stay with the FD.

Understand debt mutual fund products before you begin to use it for an emergency fund. There are several advantages to this product. It earns you a better return and is more liquid than an FD. I know some investors who, once having understood mutual funds, moved to a hybrid fund with a small equity exposure as their emergency fund. But let's wait for that conversation a bit later.

Rs 6 lakhs sounds like a lot of money for a person with a Rs 50,000 monthly expenditure, but this is the first investment you make. Set yourself a monthly target for your emergency fund and keep crediting your emergency account each month. Once you get to your target, stop funding it, and we are ready to move to more long-term investments. But before that, we need to secure the seat belt just a bit more – we need our insurances in place.

You can estimate your own emergency fund by filling the worksheet on page 218.

This is the go-to fund when disaster strikes in the form of a job loss or death. Even if you have a life cover, the money takes time to come, but the ongoing costs don't stop. I can't stress the importance of this fund. It is the difference between slipping into disaster and staying afloat.

**You are doing okay if**

1. you have six months' to two years' living costs in an emergency fund;
2. you are a double-income family with no dependent parents and have three months' living expenses;
3. you are a single-income home with dependent parents and have a year's living costs in an emergency fund; and
4. you are in your 50s and have two years of living expenses in this fund; and
5. your emergency fund sits in fixed deposits or very safe debt funds.

# EMERGENCIES NEED A FUND

## WHAT IS AN EMERGENCY FUND FOR?

**PLANNED EVENTS** ✗
- Buying a car
- Down payment of house
- Vacations

**UNPLANNED EVENTS** ✓
- Job loss
- Medical issue
- Disability or health issue
- Calamity
- Accident repairs

Fear of an emergency drives people to keep all their assets in near liquid deposits in banks

## HOW MUCH SHOULD ONE HAVE IN THE EMERGENCY FUND?

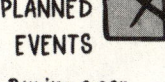

**6 to 24 MONTHS OF LIVING COST**

SPEND-IT Account

Your living cost = amount of money you transfer to your SPEND-IT ACCOUNT every month.

## WHERE SHOULD YOU KEEP THIS FUND?

BEGINNERS •————————• ADVANCED

⇒ FIXED DEPOSITS ⇒ SHORT-TERM DEBT FUNDS ⇒ CONSERVATIVE HYBRID FUNDS

**HOW**

• **Step 1:**
- Set a monthly TARGET

• **Step 2:**
- Transfer this amount to your emegency fund

• **Step 3:**
- Once you reach the goal amount, stop funding it & move to longer term investments

# 4

# BUILDING YOUR PROTECTION

*You don't want to discover you have the wrong policy when you reach the hospital. Difficult to negotiate, buying a medical cover is crucial to the health of your money box.*

I remember meeting a colleague some years back who'd been missing for a week. 'Had a nice holiday?' I asked enviously. 'Nope,' he said, 'medical emergency – mum had a stroke.' And then he cracked up. All through the hospital stay, he said, he was replaying what I would keep telling him over and over: You must have a medical cover.

He said he meant to do it but kept putting it off. He was also banking on the workplace cover he thought covered him and his dependents. But he realized at the hospital that the company, in an austerity move, had reduced the cover to his nuclear family and chucked out his dependent parents from the group cover.

He dipped into his savings, of course. But the thought that the entire expense running into several lakhs of rupees could have come out of a policy left him really upset. It's like discovering you've forgotten your mobile charger just as you step into the aircraft for a week-long trip, he said. It's that 'Oh shoot!' moment in your life.

It isn't just journalists who don't buy cover, a roomful of financial-sector CEOs once admitted to not having cover. It was the annual *Mint* Mutual Fund event and before the event began we were sitting in the antechamber waiting for the hall to fill. CEOs and CIOs (chief investment officers) of mutual funds were there as were some other senior finance professionals. Talk turned to medical cover and I went around the room asking how many people had their own cover, not the one given by the company, but their own. Shamefacedly they all admitted that they were meaning to get one, but had been stalling it. Sure, some of them are rich enough not to need a cover, but they said, it has been on their must-buy list, but they somehow never got around to it.

## What is a medical cover?

Each time we go to the doctor for a viral fever, we don't really think of the cost too much. The fee is affordable because we choose our doctors given our own spending power. The prescription medicines he gives also don't break the monthly budget. But when you have something more serious, like a surgery for a liver infection or a heart attack or a knee replacement, the costs can be significant.

One way to pay for these costs is to dip into your savings. We do hoard money in our bank deposits to take care of just such an emergency, don't we? But if we transfer this risk to somebody else for a small fee, then we don't need to dip into our investments. This transfer of the risk happens when you buy a medical insurance plan where, for the price of a premium, you buy a much larger 'cover' or insurance. You get refunded for what you spend and do not get the entire cover you have. If you have a Rs 5 lakh cover policy and your hospital bill comes to Rs 2 lakhs, you should get a refund of Rs 2 lakhs.

*Getting a good medical cover is probably more important than buying life insurance – you're more likely to go to hospital with an illness or accident than die.* But identifying this 'good' policy is so difficult.

Consider this: There are more than thirty companies that offer you a medical cover. Each company has at least ten policy choices. Each policy has further options you need to choose from. In terms of time, were you to read through all the brochures and details of all the products in the market, it would take forever. The scale of the problem freezes us. Remember, the problem is big; we are not stupid.

## Do I need cover? My office covers me

Yes, you do. I always recommend buying your own policy even if you are covered by your office, especially if you are in your forties. A double insurance cover from the offices of two working spouses when you are in your thirties does look enough. That's what techies Anmol and Richa Das thought – together they had over Rs 15,00,000 worth of medical cover from their offices.

But then things changed overnight. They had a baby; Richa left work to bring up her baby; and when cute baby Vinayak was just one, Anmol got laid off from his software firm. Luckily the story has a good ending with no major illness during the unemployment period.

The need for personal cover comes and stands in front of you when suddenly you are faced with a change in circumstances. The other time you see reality biting is at retirement. Along with the farewell party, you bid farewell to your medical cover from work. Getting a cover at age sixty is difficult. Lifestyle diseases like hypertension and diabetes may have set in, reducing the choice set of available medical plans.

Companies are reluctant to cover older people, and for older people with a 'pre-existing' disease, the reluctance is even stronger. Also, many insurance companies will not cover your 'pre-existing' diseases and medical costs related to a pre-existing disease for a maximum of four years.

Suppose you have kidney stones when you take the cover and six months after the cover you go in for a surgery to remove the stones, your medical policy will not cover the costs of this surgery.

Of course, if you are covered by the government or any other agency, even post retirement, like army and government officials are, you don't need medical cover.

## How much do I need?

A private equity investor who invests in the hospital business I spoke to sometime back had interesting insights on hospitals in the north and south of India. He finds it difficult to invest in most north Indian chains due to the conflict-of-interest issues between making undue profits off patients by ordering not-needed tests, or putting in a stent when the guy comes with gas in the belly, and giving adequate and cost-effective healthcare.

Some of the South Indian hospitals he has investments in, he said, are turning a profit, but profit is not the only motivator. You can take a flight to Trichy from Delhi, get the surgery and back, and it will still be cheaper, he said. Medical costs are insane in the five-star hospitals that the urban mass affluent now frequent.

This little story tells you why the question 'How much cover do I need?' depends on where you live, and what kind of hospital you want to go to, and what kind of privacy concerns you may have. For example, the room rent in an upmarket south Delhi hospital for a single deluxe room is upwards of Rs 10,000 a night. A less posh nursing home less than 1.5km away costs one-fourth of that.

But we can still work with some rules of thumb. You need a basic cover of Rs 3–15 lakhs per person. Use the Rs 3 lakh number for smaller towns and less posh facilities, and the Rs 15 lakh number for metros and all the bells and whistles. For a nuclear family it makes sense to get a product called a 'family floater' that allows the insurance cover to whichever member of the family that needs it.

For example, if you have a Rs 15 lakh family floater medical cover for a family of four – father, mother and two kids – any or all of them can use the cover in case of a hospitalization. For the years in which you make no claim, the outflow of premium feels heavier and heavier. But it takes one stint in hospital to see the usefulness of the premium you have paid.

## What policy do I buy?

That's the most difficult question of all, and one that everybody wants an answer to. But there are no easy answers. I'm no newbie in finance, but I have to tell you that when I was in the market to buy a policy, I had to call a financial planner.

The complexity of products, their features and the fine print in policies is so large that it is impossible for an average person to know enough to buy a policy. Most personal finance advice on this usually begins with: 'Research the company, its management, its hospital reach, its third-party agent (TPA) service (TPAs are firms that insurance companies outsource claims management to), its claims experience before you buy a policy.'

You need to know that some policies will not pay the full amount because you signed up for something called 'co-pay'. Not exactly helpful! Few articles will tell you that you need to know that some polices have in-built limits to what you can spend on what part of a hospital's service. You need to know how good the claims experience of the company is. You need to know if the TPA service is good or not. If the hospital network is large or not.

Look, it is not humanly possible to do all that and then do your day job and cook the evening meal. The problem is deep and wide, which is why there are insurance ratings available to help you choose. But some ratings can be compromised due to conflicts of interest, so take that as a starting point, but use the material in this chapter to ask questions and do your own due diligence.

As you look at the ratings online, the most important thing to know is that the cheapest policy is not necessarily a good plan. Agreed that a low premium is good and an important factor in your choice of a policy, but it is not the only factor. Look at the policy as a three-part decision.

One, how does it perform on the metric of price. Two, how does it perform on the metric of benefits. Three, how does it perform on the metric of claims. You may have the cheapest policy with the best benefits, but if the company's claims policy rejects a large number of claims, the policy is not of much use.

Let's unpack this a bit. It gets a bit technical, so stay with me. Don't go away. It is important that you spend time now rather than crib later.

## Price

It is important to know what the policy costs right now and in the future. Unlike a life cover, where your premium gets locked when you buy a term cover, the premium of a medical cover changes as we age. You need to look at two things in price. How does the price compare with policies from other companies right now and how does the price compare over the years? Your policy may cost the least today but may become the most expensive when you hit age sixty or seventy.

If you are buying from an agent, ask him to show you the price comparison at ten-year differences. If you are forty, ask for the price of the policy as it is today when sold to a fifty-, sixty- and seventy-year-old. If he can't do the work, find another agent. He will be getting a commission on your purchase now and every year after you buy. Let him earn this commission by doing the work that you want him to do. Don't get distracted by the sales spiel.

## Benefits

We buy a medical cover so that when faced with a hospital bill we don't have to dip into our savings. The deal is simple: You pay an annual premium and when you get hospitalized, the insurance company pays the bill. But then it is a complicated world. Insurance companies have the ability to set up the game so that you lose. And given how technical an insurance product is, there is no way you will know all that there is to know. You need to find out if your policy gives at least these eight benefits.

One, *ensure that you have a policy that does not have something called a 'co-pay' clause.* This is called 'co-pay' because you agree to pay a certain percentage of a bill to share the costs with the insurance company. Unfair, you exclaim. It is, except when a senior citizen goes to buy a cover, co-pay allows him to at least get a cover. More of that later. For example, if you agree to a co-pay of 10 per cent, you have agreed to pick up one-tenth of the cost of the hospitalization. If your bill is Rs 2 lakhs, you will have to pay Rs 20,000 and the insurance company will pay 90 per cent or Rs 1.8 lakhs.

Look for a policy that does not have a co-pay clause. Ask your agent to mail you the policy document and then do a search on the words co-pay. Search the net to see if the policy being sold has complaints related to it having a co-pay clause. Build an email trail with the company or the agent to ensure that you have something in writing that ensures that you have not been lied to. The presence of an evil co-pay clause has caused plenty of curses to fly in the direction of insurance companies when the glitzy promises of care turn into castles of sand at the time of a health crisis.

Two, *check for a 'pre-existing' disease clause*. Insurance companies will not cover diseases that you already have when you take the policy. Insurance rules allow a company to refuse to pay for any treatment related to any condition, ailment or injury for which you were diagnosed or had symptoms when you took the policy, for four years.

For example, if you were diagnosed with kidney stones and took a policy soon after, the company is within its rights not to pay for the surgery to remove those stones if it happens in the next four years. But there are companies that waive or reduce this waiting period, to pay up earlier. Check to see how long the waiting period is in the policy you shortlist.

But a caveat here: People with any pre-existing disease find it difficult to get a cover. Some insurance companies use this clause to refuse claims for totally unrelated ailments. It is a good idea to disclose your correct present and past medical history to the insurance company when you sign up for the policy. Else they will have a tool in their hands to refuse your claim. And, believe me, they use it to refuse claims on very flimsy grounds.

One columnist for *Mint* documented how a pregnant lady was hospitalized for fever. Normally the fever may not have needed hospitalization, but because she was pregnant, she was admitted. The claim was rejected because ailments related to pregnancy are not covered in the policy.

Three, *check if your policy has a 'disease waiting period'*. Many companies have a cool-off period of thirty to ninety days during which they will not pay any claim. Some ailments such as cataract or hernia may have a 'waiting period' before the company will pay. Ask the agent to list out all diseases that are covered under this clause. Look for a policy that does not have a waiting period on diseases or coverage.

Four, *check if your policy has 'sub-limits'*. A friend was admitted for a knee surgery to one of Delhi's upmarket hospitals. Confident of a Rs 4 lakh cover, she selected a single deluxe room. When the time for the payout came, the insurance company refused to pay the room rent, which was over Rs 4,000 a day. Her policy had a sub-limit of 1 per cent, which is the portion of the cover that can be spent on room rent. Her cover was Rs 4 lakhs, so her room rent over Rs 4,000 a day was not paid by the policy. Other expenses were also paid in line with a Rs 4,000-room, reducing the claim amount even more as some hospitals hike charges according to room rent.

You need to check this carefully. A sub-limit is a limitation on what the company will pay out for specific things. We usually stumble upon a sub-limit on room rent. There are two kinds of limits on room rents – either by price or by category. Your policy may say that it will pay a maximum of Rs 2,000 as room rent or it may say that you are eligible for a double occupancy room with air conditioning. Room rents in the large five-star health shops (can't call them hospitals any more) cost much more. Remember that the other expenses are associated with the type of room you take. You could find yourself paying for a lot more if you take a higher category room than what your policy will pay for. Look for a policy with no sub-limits.

Five, *check for exclusions*. A policy will list out diseases, conditions and medical services that the policy does not cover. Dental treatment, pregnancy and cosmetic surgery are standard exclusions. It is a good idea to get a list of all that is excluded in the policy you buy. What you can't do much about is when the policy you buy excludes something at some future point in the policy. One firm excluded a costly cancer injection midway in a policy and people who bought the plan and made a claim were not paid for that injection. The dice is loaded against us, the individual customers of mediclaim.

Six, *ask how much of the costs before and after hospitalization the policy will cover*. You can claim expenditure made on doctor's fees, medicines and diagnostic tests done before a planned hospitalization and for three months afterwards. For example, a knee replacement will have MRI costs before the surgery and physiotherapy costs post surgery. Check if you can claim these costs. Check the exact amount and time your policy will cover.

Seven, *ask for a list of 'day-care' procedures that don't need you to stay for twenty-four hours in a hospital any more*. Procedures and treatment such as a cataract surgery or surgery for a ligament tear (there is a standard list of 130 such procedures) are treated as 'day-care' procedures and are covered. Check the details of the day-care clause, what will be covered, how much will be paid and how long you have to stay to claim.

Eight, *look at the 'no-claims bonus' feature*. When you don't make a claim in a year, you get rewarded by the insurance company. It does this by giving a 'no-claims bonus' (NCB). The usual way is to raise your cover by 10 per cent for the same premium. If your cover was Rs 15 lakhs, for a premium of Rs 25,000, when you have a claim-free year, you get a cover of Rs 16.5 lakhs for the same premium.

## Claims

Your search for that good policy is not over till you understand the claims history of the company you finally choose. You know if a telecom service is good or not when you use it. It is very here and now, but for a medical policy, the moment of truth is at the hospital door or when you file a claim. Does the insurer pay up? How much does he pay? Is the process easy? How quickly does the company respond to complaints?

These are questions that you must think about at the time of buying your policy. Unfortunately, in India, claims data is not standardized and is difficult to get. The regulator has not thought the disclosure of data through so as to make it meaningful to consumers. Ask the agents these questions on claims before you buy.

One, *how many claims does the company settle?* Out of 100, if the company's claims history does not settle more than ninety-five claims, don't buy from the firm. Claims are a tricky area because the companies club together group and individual claims data. Group claims get paid far more than individual claims. Ideally the disclosure on claims should be product-wise and not clubbed as one big number.

Two, *look at the claim-complaints data and look for a policy that has less than thirty complaints on every 10,000 claims made.* Be careful of firms that give data on complaints as a percentage of policies sold. What is relevant is how many people, how many made a claim, then how many went on to complain. This number should be low in the policy you finally choose.

Yup, you need a degree in finance, law and patience to choose a mediclaim policy. You could just look at the different ratings online if you find this process too complicated. Your exact policy type or need may not be in the ratings, but if you look at the parameters, you will get this data for the company. And don't forget to speak with a financial planner as well. Who said choosing a medical policy is easy?

## What to do if you are not getting cover because of a pre-existing disease?

A colleague wrote to me some time back. He had an angioplasty twelve years ago, but finds it difficult to get a cover even after a disease-free period of more than a decade. Insurance companies ideally want to insure supermen and superwomen who are in the best of health and won't ever make a claim. Some companies take their aversion to giving cover to people with a pre-existing ailment to ridiculous lengths. If you fall in this category and are not getting cover, there are still some things you can do.

You can buy a policy with sub-limits, co-pay and an exclusion period for your existing ailment. Remember sub-limits are limits on what the policy will pay for certain diseases and for the room rent and related costs. A co-pay is what you agree to share with the company in terms of cost. An exclusion period is the waiting period before the policy will start paying a claim.

These are restrictive, but better than not having a policy. Also, you may get 'loaded' or pay an amount over the regular premium paid by a healthy person due to your pre-existing ailment.

What I suggested to my colleague is this: If you are totally unable to get a policy, start a regular systematic investment in a long-term product like a hybrid mutual fund (we'll discuss this in more detail in Chapter 9) and mentally label it 'medical-cost fund'. If you were planning to buy a Rs 5 lakh cover, target a Rs 10 lakh fund for your medical costs. If you don't need the fund and stay healthy, this is money that you will bequeath to your kids.

## Strategies for older people

Many people who are over sixty-five are sitting on Rs 1–3 lakh of medical covers. Bought in the era of lower medical costs and no five-star hospitals, these are quite inadequate for the current medical costs. We know that insurance companies resist insuring older people. What to do? The best way to get a larger cover is to use what is called a 'top-up' plan.

Think of this as a policy that will pay up after a certain threshold amount has been paid by you. Suppose you have an existing policy for Rs 3 lakh medical cover. Now you buy a top-up plan that gives you another Rs 5 lakhs of cover, but after a Rs 3 lakh deductible. If your medical bill is Rs 4 lakhs, you will pay Rs 3 lakhs from your basic policy and Rs 1 lakh from your top-up.

Even if you get admitted twice, with Rs 2 lakhs your bill each time, your costs still will be covered. Remember to buy a top-up that allows you to claim after the deductible is covered across different episodes in hospital. If you are unable to get even a top-up, targeting your own medical fund is your only option. Talk to your kids if you don't have the surplus. Many of them will be able to get you on to their work-given group health insurance plans.

**Critical illness and personal accident**

Do I buy a critical illness and accident cover while I'm at it? Yes, you do. A critical illness, like cancer, is a disease where you may not spend too much time in hospital but have very large out-of-pocket expenses. The disease may also affect your ability to work for some time. Such illnesses are covered by a 'critical illness' cover. These policies pay a lump sum if you get any of the illness that are part of the contract.

Some policies cover up to twenty such illnesses including cancer, kidney failure, heart attack, major organ transplant, stroke, serious burns and end-stage diseases of the liver and lung. A Rs 10 lakh policy should cost between Rs 3,000 and Rs 5,000 roughly. Prices will change and differ according to company, features and the person buying the plan.

You should be able to add a 'rider' to your existing policy on the policy renewal date. A rider is an add-on at a very low cost to a basic policy. Riders look attractive, but I recommend that you buy a stand-alone accident policy from a general insurer. This cover is likely to be more comprehensive and will not lapse if you discontinue your basic policy for any reason.

A personal accident policy adds another layer of security to your by-now robust medical insurance portfolio. This kind of policy gives you a lump sum if you meet with an accident that leaves you temporarily or permanently disabled. A personal accident plan has four covers: death, permanent disability, permanent partial disability and temporary total disability.

For death or permanent disability, the policy pays the entire sum assured. For permanent partial disability, the policy pays a part of the sum assured, and for temporary total disability, it pays a weekly compensation, usually up to 104 weeks.

How much insurance you buy depends on how insecure you feel about your health and the future. An old wise uncle, now deceased, once told me that we all need to decide what level of safety makes us feel safe. Do you need a helmet or a seat belt on the road or do you need an armoured car? The answer will depend on who you are and what danger you perceive, and what you are able to afford.

I know, you're tired of reading. And I'm tired of putting down all there is to buying a medical plan. It is tough. There are too many moving parts. You can use the health insurance ratings to shortlist some products, but the best solution will be to work with a good financial planner to buy your medical plan. Use the information here to see if the planner knows more than you or not. If you don't hear the words pre-existing, sub-limits, claims and waiting periods, you know that you need to keep searching.

You can make out from the tone of this part of the book how deeply I distrust insurance firms. This comes from years of getting complaints from people who have been trapped and cheated. It comes from decoding products and finding a problem of intent in lots of them.

The intent is not to pay. Your best bet is to work with a good planner or insurance agent who has clout with the company. As an individual, there is literally nothing much you can do. Our healthcare system is broken. Both public and private. I shudder when people grandly look at privatization of the public health system in India as a solution to healthcare. They don't seem to understand that without proper regulation of both hospitals and insurance firms, you are herding people from one disaster to another.

You need a medical cover more than you need a life insurance cover since you are more likely to break a leg than die. This cover is the difference between using your savings for a medical emergency and simply flashing your cashless card.

**You are doing okay if**

1. along with your work cover, you have your own family floater;
2. you live in small-town India, and have a family floater between Rs 3 and 7 lakhs;
3. you live in the large metros, and want the five-star hospitals, and have a minimum of Rs 15 lakhs' family floater; and
4. you are over sixty years old and have a top-up plan to bump up your basic cover.

# MEDICAL EMERGENCIES NEED A COVER

**HAVE A PERSONAL MEDICAL COVER!**

OFFICE COVERS ARE GOOD UNTIL A JOB LOSS OR RETIREMENT

## HOW MUCH DO YOU NEED?

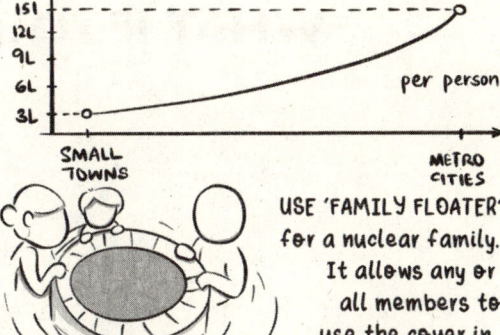

15L, 12L, 9L, 6L, 3L — per person — SMALL TOWNS ... METRO CITIES

USE 'FAMILY FLOATER' for a nuclear family. It allows any or all members to use the cover in case of a need.

### WHICH POLICY TO BUY?

look at the policy as a three-part decision:

PRICE • BENEFIT • CLAIMS

 **PRICE:** Know what the policy costs now & in the future. SEE THE PRICE COMPARISON AT TEN-YEAR DIFFERENCES.

## BENEFITS TO CHECK FOR:

- **NO CO-PAY**
- **NO PRE-EXISTING DISEASE CLAUSE** — DISCLOSE ALL THE MEDICAL HISTORY!
- **NO 'DISEASE WAITING PERIOD.'** AVOID IT!
- **LIMITS** — THERE ARE LIMITATIONS ON WHAT THE COMPANY WILL PAY FOR SPECIFIC THINGS
- **CHECK FOR EXCLUSIONS** — PREGNANCY NOT COVERED!!
- **HOW MUCH OF THE COSTS WILL POLICY COVER BEFORE & AFTER HOSPITALIZATION?**
- **ALL THE DAY-CARE PROCEDURES THAT ARE COVERED**
- **NO-CLAIMS BONUS FEATURE**

Don't buy if the company does not settle 95+ out of every 100 claims!

Look for a policy that has less than 30 complaints on every 10,000 claims made

Check with your AGENT for this information

# 5

# WHAT IF YOU DIE?

*We buy life insurance for all the wrong reasons – fear, greed, pity, frustration, taxes. The real reason for a life cover, to protect your family if you die, is never explained.*

Kanchan Chander is a famous Delhi-based artist; you can spot her on page 3 of the daily tabloids grinning at the camera. I happened to meet her at the home of a common friend. And as it played out, the conversation soon shifted to her money. (There was not much I knew about art anyway.)

She was in the middle of a story that I had now heard hundreds of times. A pushy bank relationship manager promises a wonder insurance-cum-investment product; you trust your bank; you grew up in a time when insurance meant safety and good return, along with tax breaks. This relationship manager is very persuasive, calls many times, is very charming, looks sincerely into your eyes and gives his personal promise about the product; I'm there, he says.

Kanchan's story was no different. She wanted to put away a lump sum for two years so that she could fund her son's art-school education in the UK. However, she was sold a fifteen-year regular-premium unit-linked insurance plan some years ago by her bank. She thought she was buying a two-year fixed deposit, but the bank had put her in a regular-premium long-term investment. She got a shock when a year later she got a message from the insurance company saying that the second premium is due.

But, she had made a one-time investment, she thought. So she called her bank relationship manager. He had gone. Another smart slick-suit was there who told her that if she did not make the payment she'd lose the entire investment to costs (which she was not told at the time of investment). She protested. You signed the policy, so you should have known this, was the pushback. Kanchan was devastated. Artists' incomes are erratic and she had been banking on this money to fund her son's education, and now it was gone. As a single parent, the blow was even harder. There was nobody to fall back upon.

Chances are that you've already had at least one bad insurance experience by now. Either you would have got back a pittance after faithfully servicing your policy for twenty years, or you would have got trapped in a product you did not want. Or been brazenly lied to and left holding a dud product. Why do they cheat and what can you do to stay safe?

Do you really need an insurance cover? What about the tax break – how will you get that if you don't buy another policy?

I'm going to take each question and then leave you with some very simple dos and don'ts. You need to treat the insurance industry and those who sell the same as walking through reptile-infested waters; you need to stay on the path that is safe. They're out to get you. You need to look after your money. I'm not joking.

## Why you need a life cover

Not to save taxes, not for a secure retirement, not because the ad agency put together images of happy families doing cool things together. Not because you are arm-twisted into buying a policy by a family member, a friend, a neighbour, your bank or just a very won't-take-no-for-an-answer agent.

One night I got a call from Richa Agnihotri, a friend. She used to teach physics at that time and is nobody's fool, not the usual I-can't-do-numbers person at all. But that day she sounded a bit hysterical. 'He's not going, Monika. Will you talk to him?'

'He' was the insurance agent the family had bought dud policies from for over twenty years. Now, my friend was in the process of shifting to a financial planner and was refusing to buy; the point at which a desperate Richa called me was when he had simply refused to leave their house till they bought a policy. He had invoked past relationships, threatened to tell her mother-in-law (I kid you not!).

I got on the phone and tried to discuss the policy he was selling, asking questions on returns and cover. It was a poor plan that gave a thin cover and returns that did worse than a bank FD. As I pushed back, he realized that his game was over. Probably mentally hurling abuses at me, he left. Richa now works with a planner and has finally moved the dud plans out of her portfolio.

I can recount story after story of the hard push of life-insurance products. Another lady was sold dud plans out of her retirement funds by an ex-student. A driver who worked with me some years back was sold a lemon by his past employer. The contractor who built my house says his bank manager each year makes him buy several three-year insurance plans.

Possibly the most difficult to say no to are the people you know very well. If you want to benefit somebody, give them money for nothing. Please don't give this donation or charity respect by making it a financial transaction where you get something in return. In fact, you lose not just this money, but subsequent premiums to a product that does not work for you. You are harming your financial future and that of your family by doing this 'charity'. You lose both the money and the relationship.

You need a life insurance cover for *only* one reason: *to protect your family's financial health if you die an untimely death*.

Shut your eyes for a moment and imagine not being there. Being dead. Seriously, do it. You may have seen your loved ones crying, coming to terms with you not being around.

After the emotional trauma, you see the financial vulture land on the house.

You see your spouse wondering what will happen to them now that your salary that paid the EMI is gone. Will the car, also on an EMI, be returned too? Your teenage kids are grown up enough to realize that their plans to go abroad are suddenly only a dream. Work may have to begin much earlier than they thought. There is a grainy grimness about the future. About bills and fees and stuff that only you carried on your shoulder.

When I did this exercise, my overwhelming thought was to reach out from beyond the dead and help the family out. To point where the papers are kept; to whisper passwords they were searching for; to go and punch Yama in the face and say, 'It wasn't my time yet, I still had to fix my family's future. And eat that mango kulfi falooda that I'd been salivating for so long. And just finish that last episode of *Better Call Saul!*' Oh well. Nice to open the eyes!

When you die an untimely death, you leave lots of things midway – it could be a meal, sleep, a conversation, a fight, a joke, a holiday plan. You also leave your family midway in their journey through life – both physically and financially.

While we can work on leaving only good memories with our family by becoming the person we think we are, the financial piece is much easier to do. You need to figure out how much the family will need to live, without you bringing in the monthly income, and how much for the future of the kids' education and marriage. You may have dependent parents and a spouse who does not earn, and may need to provide for them till they are alive as well. Think of this as just income replacement – how big a lump sum (that will earn a return) do you need today so that your income will not be missed by the family if you are not around.

The other big expense that will hit the family if you suddenly disappear is the debt you have. Home loans, car loans, education, personal loans, credit card debt – all of this will need to be paid back if you are to continue using what was bought with a loan. While some banks may be sympathetic in such cases, do you really want that pressure on your family when the problem can be easily resolved? You need a life insurance cover to look after all of these expenses and costs if your lifeline is cut before time.

You'd have realized by now that we're looking at a very large sum as the life insurance cover. Add up the cover (look in the policies you have and add up the figure under 'sum assured') you have in all your existing policies and see how much your life insurance cover is – not the value of the policy when it matures, but what the beneficiary gets if you die.

The way insurance has been sold in India, my guess is that you are sitting on a lot of dud policies. Why do I call them 'dud'? Because they don't solve any of your financial problems. These are products not designed to give you either a good cover or a good return. In its purest form, a life insurance cover should pay your beneficiary a lump sum when you die for the price of the premium. If you outlive your policy, no money comes back.

Think of the premium as the price of the product. Ask the question, what am I getting for this price? If you can't answer the question clearly, you don't have a term plan. A pure life insurance policy is called a 'term plan'. This is not a policy that your agent or bank will tell you about. Why? Because it is cheap and does not soak up too much of your money.

An average thirty-five-year-old can buy a twenty-five-year term plan that gives his beneficiary Rs 1 crore (Rs 10 million) if he dies within those twenty-five years for the price of Rs 8,000 to 10,000 a year. Pull out your plans and see how much cover you have. I can assure you that if you don't have a term plan, you don't have much cover. You have a dud. Or many, many duds.

## Understanding life insurance products in the market

In a term policy, your premium is a price you pay for buying a life cover. So if your premium is Rs 10,000 a year for a one-crore cover, this is the price you pay to the insurance company for taking the risk of you dying an untimely death. When you buy this policy, you understand that if you live beyond the policy term (usually till you reach retirement age – more of this in the chapter on retirement), you get nothing back. Your Rs 10,000 a year for twenty to thirty years is a 'waste'. You got nothing back.

This is where you need to rework your own belief about this being a 'waste'. It is not. It is the price you pay for buying a life cover. You hope that your family does not have to collect the insurance and that you die of old age.

It is easier to see the logic of why we should 'waste' this money on a term policy than buy the other kinds of policies in the market – endowment, money-back plans or unit-linked policies – once we understand how these policies work.

The typical endowment insurance policy gives you a tiny crust of life insurance cover; it is usually ten times your premium. So if your premium is Rs 50,000 a year, your life cover is Rs 5 lakhs. It also promises to give you a return on your money. And that is the carrot for you – you get a 'cover', so your family's safe; you get a return and you get a tax break. The pista on the jalebi is that the money at maturity is tax-free.

The way the policy is sold talks about the returns in terms of whole numbers: You invest Rs 50,000 a year for five years and you get back Rs 5 lakhs after another fifteen years. Or you invest Rs 50,000 a year for fifteen years and you get back Rs 10 lakhs.

The whole numbers look big with lots of zeros, but ask the question what the return percentage a year is, and you get shocking answers. The first policy returns 4.15 per cent a year. The second, 3.98 per cent a year. Sometimes the pitch is even more complicated. I really do get the impression that the intention is to obfuscate and hide the real return of the product in fancy numbers.

*An easy way to cut through the tyranny of being hit by large numbers is to use the Rule of 72.* This is a versatile rule that we shall use many times in the book. To know the rate of return every year of a double-your-money proposition, simply ask the question: Over what time does my money double? Then divide 72 by that number.

Suppose the agent says: Your Rs 1 lakh will grow to Rs 2 lakhs in fifteen years, divide 72 by 15. Your return per year is 4.8 per cent, which is near the 4.73 number that a more exact calculation will give.

Over the past decades that I tracked this industry, my team and I decoded hundreds of these policies to find out what they finally return as a percentage of your investment. If we are smart enough to understand that an FD gives back an interest of 6 or 7 per cent, why then does an insurance policy hide this return so carefully?

The reason is that they give you pathetic returns. On an average, a guaranteed return policy gives around 3 per cent annual return. What are called participating plans (or plans that give you a 'bonus' at the end of the policy) give between 0.5 per cent to 4 per cent return. You read that correctly.

At a *Mint* event, we had invited a senior official of the insurance regulator. He spoke about a policy that the regulator itself had decoded and found a return of 0.5 per cent a year after ten years. As an aside: The use of the word 'bonus' is meant to trigger that part of your brain that wants an extra thing for free. But it is not a 'bonus' in the real sense of the word. It is your return.

It is like a bank FD saying: Hey dude, you get a bonus. We not only return your money you invested at the end of the year, but even give you a 7 per cent bonus on it! Just as calling 'interest' a 'bonus' is silly, so is calling a return that the policy gives a 'bonus' bizarre. But that's the Indian insurance industry for you. They feed off your trust and willingness to believe in their bad products.

A lot of people make the mistake of thinking that the poor returns are because of the life insurance cover. Think of the premium as a price again. This price is now buying you two things: an insurance cover and a return. The price of an insurance cover (called mortality price) cannot be different for the same person for a term policy and for a bundled policy because it is based on what are called 'actuarial tables'. Let's not worry about jargon here, but just understand that the price of your pure life cover is calculated by keeping in mind, among other things, how long an average person lives, what the gender is and at what age they are today.

So now we know that the price of the pure risk cover should be the same across a term policy and an endowment policy. Now let's look at the price of two similar cover plans. If the premium of Rs 1,000 a year buys a thirty-five-year-old person a life cover of Rs 5 lakhs for twenty-five years in a term plan, then the cost should be the same in the money-back plan of the life cover, right?

This means that of the Rs 50,000 a year premium in a bundled product, just Rs 1,000 is going towards your life cover. The bulk – that is Rs 49,000 a year – is your investment.

The day I understood this, the world stopped for a moment. I pulled out the junk policies I'd been sold over the years to see what the damage was. Huge. Endowment plans destroy wealth over the long term. *The day you realize that it is in your best interest to separate your investment and insurance products is the day you move solidly towards building your financial security*. Else you are building wealth for the seller and the insurance companies.

Two things go wrong when you buy a bundled product. One, the cover you get is pathetically small. If you can pay an annual premium of Rs 50,000, it is reasonable to assume that your annual income must be at least Rs 6 lakhs. If you die tomorrow, what will Rs 5 lakhs do for your family as an insurance payout? Nothing. Zilch. How much should you have bought? At least Rs 60 lakhs – the 'why this much' will get answered in the next section. But let's just stay with this for a moment longer. What will a Rs 60 lakh cover cost you in terms of premium if you insist on buying this bundled product? About Rs 6 lakhs as premium. Or exactly equal to your annual income! I told you. These plans are terrible.

Why do they get sold so hard? Because of the way the incentive structure is built into life insurance in India. The first-year commission (in 2024 for a more than 11 years regular premium traditional policy) can be up to 100 per cent of your premium. For Rs 1 lakh that you invest, the entire first premium can go to the agent who pushes the policy at you. This is the legal payment.

While 100 per cent commissions may not be the norm, but first-year commissions do go upto 75 per cent in many cases. Those are the stakes of you continuing to buy these dud plans. Don't you get sold newer products each year in insurance? Now you know why. The first-year commission is the big ladoo every agent is after. Who cares about policy servicing or annual renewal once the first premium is in the bag. The subsequent commissions fall to 7.5 per cent.

What about ULIPs?* Think of a ULIP (unit-linked insurance plan) as a mutual fund with a crust of insurance on top of it. ULIPs used to be really toxic products till 2010 but since then have become much better in terms of costs. But they still have problems of poor portfolio disclosure and lack of portability, making them not such great vehicles for investment. *I prefer to unbundle my investment from my insurance, and stay with a large term plan for my life insurance needs, and buy mutual funds for my investment.* How large is a large cover?

## How much cover do I need?

If you died today, think of all the expenses that the family has ahead of them. Now think of how much they will need to put

---

* India had the 'traditional' version of a life insurance policy till 2001, where you bought a money-back or endowment policy. Once the insurance industry opened up to private firms, a new market-linked version was introduced called a unit-linked insurance plan. This kind of an insurance plan gives the option to the investor to invest in stocks or bonds, or a combination of both. The fat commission for a first-time sale and a booming stock market gave rise to the big ULIP scam in India.

away in a fixed deposit or a tax-free bond or a mutual fund to generate a regular income? The rule of thumb is that *you need eight to ten times your take-home annual income*. Or fifteen to twenty times your annualized monthly expenditure.

Let's work with some numbers. Suppose your annual take-home income is Rs 12 lakhs, or about Rs 1 lakh a month. You die. Your cover was for a nice fat Rs 1.2 crore. Your spouse gets this money. She does not understand bonds or funds and just puts this in a 6 per cent ten-year fixed deposit (FD); she is able to generate Rs 60,000 a month. Remember, not the entire sum of Rs 1 lakh was consumed; there was a part that was getting saved. Of course, we're assuming that you did not die penniless and had other investments and had your provident fund in place that she gets to invest as well.

In addition to a cover for your income, you need to buy insurance for all the debt you have. Each time you take a large loan – usually a home loan, sometimes a personal loan – buy a term cover for the full amount of the loan that you take. Suppose you take a home loan of Rs 80 lakhs. Buy a term cover of Rs 80 lakhs. Your bank may offer you a reducing cover policy whose premium is bundled with your EMI. Say no. It's likely to be more expensive and there is another logic for buying a Rs 80 lakh cover. As your loan amount falls, you are growing older, doing better at your work. Your salary is rising; therefore the need for the cover is rising.

## When's a good time to buy?

*Buy as soon as you have dependents or the possibility of getting dependents arises*. Typically, you will buy a life cover once you get married and have a dependent spouse. If the spouse is earning, and you have no loans, you may be able to postpone the purchase of the cover till the kids come along. Even if you are not married and plan not to marry, but carry the responsibility of an unmarried sibling or parents on your shoulders, you still need a life insurance policy.

So buy the policy the moment you realize that other people in the family will suffer financially if you die suddenly. Buy as early as possible because you get locked in for the duration of the policy from your first premium. And this is something you need to know: The younger you are, the cheaper you lock in for.

Touching thirty is usually a good time to buy the cover. You are old enough to have a good income flow and dependents, but not that old for covers to be too expensive. The cost of life cover rises exponentially as you age. A cover of Rs 1 crore for a thirty-year-old will cost between Rs 8,000–10,000 a year. For a forty-five-year-old, this cost will more than double.

Did I hear you rushing to buy for your twenty-year-old son who is still in college and is some years away from earning? You say: You just said lock in early, I'm just doing that, no? Ah ... but there needs to be an income that you are insuring! The cover you get is a multiple of what you earn.

So no income means that the chances of a large cover are slim. So, buy early, and buy cheap. But remember that you will have to revisit this decision several times over the next 25–30 years.

## What about the taxes?

Hello! But what about my tax-saving? What am I going to do for that? Lots of fish in that pond, so chill. We've been brought up to think that a life insurance premium is the only way to do tax-saving at the end of the year.

I used to get a lot of panicked calls around 15 March every year asking for what to do about making the tax-saving investment. Since there is a little bit of work to be done in on-boarding other products in the 80C basket, and the insurance agent gets a fat share of your first premium as commission, guess which is the easier to buy? Why did the panic calls stop? Friends and family got smarter. Also I think I may have snapped at some – if you ask me the same thing every year on 15 March, and then go and buy another damn policy, I'll finally snap, no? Human and all that.

You have plenty of options in the 80C basket. But for investment, you can do a special five-year bank deposit that gets you the same tax break. You can invest in the public provident fund (PPF), the National Pension Scheme (NPS) or a tax-saving mutual fund.

These mutual funds are called equity-linked savings schemes (ELSSs) and are my favourite for long-term investing while getting a tax break. We'll hear a lot more about funds in the chapter on mutual funds. In fact, this chapter became the reason I wrote my next book *Let's Talk Mutual Funds*! Of course, if you are part of the really well off, you don't need to do anything. Your provident fund contribution of up to Rs 1.5 lakhs will be taken as the tax-saving amount – giving you the same benefit as a dud insurance plan.

## Which policy to buy and how to buy it?

Now that you fully get the story – that you need a life insurance cover that is at least 8–10 times your annual take-home income, and that you need to buy *a cover that gets you till you are financially independent* – the next question stands up: What policy to buy? Are private sector insurers 'safe'?

The policy you buy is a mix of getting a cheap plan from a company that is known to honour its claims. Why cheap? Term insurance is a pure vanilla product. You pay a premium; if you die, the company hands over a fat cheque to your spouse. Since this is a long-term contract – usually a twenty- to twenty-five-year policy term (remember, we're getting you a cover till your retirement) – the cheaper you buy the better it is. Also, once you buy a policy at a particular price, you get locked into this price (unlike the medical policies in the previous chapter). Consider inflation, and the premium you pay after fifteen years is worth just half of the rupees you pay in real terms.

Rule One: *Get a cheap plan.* The online plans are the cheapest since they remove a part of the agent commission from the price of the insurance. When term plans were launched online some years ago, the prices dropped by almost half! A policy sold by an agent costs twice as much as the policy you buy online.

We changed our policies midway from an agent-bought-one to an online one some years back. We were older and we got more cover, but the online price was only a little over the price we were paying for the older policy. We let go of the old policy and bought a new one. Luckily, we've not used it. And hope that money gets 'wasted' and goes down the drain.

Rule Two: *When buying a term cover, check the claims experience of the insurance firm.* Shortlist three or four policies that you like in terms of low prices for your age, cover and tenure, and then start looking at the claims experience. This is not so easy to find. A claims experience of over 95 per cent is fine. This means that the company pays 95 per cent of the claims filed. Do a simple internet search on this metric to see which firms show up.

Are private companies safe? I've been asked this almost each time I've spoken about insurance in my public talks. What do we mean by 'safe'? Will they run away with our money? No, they won't. We have a regulator in place that sets the rules of the game. These rules say that any insurance company needs to have enough money to be solvent. Will the insurance company be around twenty years later? Well, some of them have already been in the business for more than twenty years and will be around in the future as well. If a company wants to get out of the insurance business, it will sell its shares to another company or get taken over. So, yes, it is safe to buy a term plan from any company with a claims experience of at least 95 per cent.

## Have a plan

You need to have a plan for the people left behind. Imagine this: Your spouse, who is not an active participant in the financial decisions, is suddenly hit with the trauma of you copping it early and a large lump sum hitting the bank. You need to have a plan in place that will guide her (I use 'her' deliberately because mostly it is the men who handle finances in an Indian home – mine is the exception where I worry about financial planning in the house). Let's talk about this in more detail in the chapter on wills. For those who want to action this, you can fill the *Let's Talk Legacy* planner and document your life.

## When do I not need a life cover?

If you have no dependents on your income, you don't need any life insurance cover. Let me repeat that. If there will be nobody to miss your income – *do not* buy a life insurance cover. There is one more situation in which you don't need a cover – when you are financially free. When are you financially free?

When you don't need to go to work to pay your bills, EMI, fees and other living costs. Your investments are large enough to look after all your expenses – current and future.

Most people reach this milestone around the age of sixty, when they retire. Retirement either comes with a pension or a lump sum that is invested to harvest an income.

But suppose you get very rich midway. Maybe you cash out the business you own and plan to just invest that money and not work any more, or you inherit a large estate from your parents that takes care of all your financial needs. When that happens, you don't need a life cover. What if you die? The same corpus will look after the family.

*The job of the life insurance cover is to serve you till you are debt-free and financially independent.* The moment that happens you can stop your term insurance plan. Remember that these are annual contracts; if you terminate it, you lose nothing. You lose a lot if you terminate your endowment policies midway. One more reason to just stay with a term plan.

Kanchan's story ended well. I told her how to fight back. She wrote to the US headquarters of the bank, naming the global CEO in her mail. In two weeks she had her money back. Her son went to art school in the UK and is now a budding Delhi artist and theatre person. Kanchan now works with a certified financial planner and regularly calls me up to say: Thanks, you saved my life. I feel so much in control of my life.

At the end of the chapter I will say it one more time. To protect your family against your *untimely death*, the only life insurance product you need is a *pure term cover*. Do not buy any other kind of cover. **Do not mix investment and insurance** in the same product.

You can estimate your own life insurance cover by filling the worksheet on page 220.

> A life cover is a crucial piece of your money box that allows your family to maintain their lifestyles and future goals. You have been misled about this product for decades.
>
> **You are doing okay if**
>
> 1. you have a pure term insurance plan;
> 2. you bought this online to remove agent commission cost;
> 3. you don't have a single ULIP or 'traditional' plan in your money box; and
> 4. you have a sum assured that is eight to ten times your annual take-home income or fifteen to twenty times your annual expenditure.

# 6

# FINALLY, WE'RE INVESTING

*We resist investing for many reasons. No money, concerns about safety and not knowing where to invest are just some of the excuses we make. In this chapter, we understand the right way to think about investing so that we take risk, but with a seat belt on.*

I began serious investing quite late in my life. The early years of a career are marked by tiny salaries and fairly high costs, especially if you are supporting an extended family. The years between twenty-five to thirty-five are really tough for a young couple. Marriage, kids, setting-up-your-home cost, and, in some cases, you have to look after an extended family as well. The incomes are small as this is the beginning of the career and even two-income homes find it difficult to balance all the competing needs.

I remember how difficult that public provident fund (PPF) contribution used to be at the end of the year, and how my husband and I would struggle to make it. But we were committed to making that contribution because we were both working for India's first personal finance magazine – *Intelligent Investor* (now called *Outlook Money*) – and I had worked out that Rs 5,000 a month in PPF over thirty years would make me a crorepati.

Back in those days, PPF used to give 12 per cent and the value of a crore was a much, much bigger deal than it is today. Remember, in the 1990s, a 2 BHK (bedroom, hall and kitchen) in South Delhi cost just Rs 25–30 lakhs. Those were the years that the tax-saving investment was the only investment we could afford to make. And there were years in which we could not make the maximum Rs 70,000 investment for the year. And then, even that came down over the next few years because I took a financially risky call.

The early years are tougher for young mothers. I went right back to work after my maternity leave – the family needed the money. But by the time our daughter was a year old, I could see that it really upset her to see me leave for work. I too could not focus fully on work thinking about her missing me. It got to a stage where I decided to quit and look after the baby. We were moving cities with my husband in a new and slightly better-paying job, and I decided to go cold turkey and quit. I still remember that feeling of stepping off a cliff. *BA kiya hai, MA kiya. Lagta hai ye sab yu hi kiya.*

A bachelor's from Shri Ram College of Commerce, master's from Delhi School of Economics and a second master's, in journalism, from the UK – and I'm going full-time mom! Many of my girlfriends were not impressed. Some work-related friends stopped talking to me thinking that my career was over. We went from a two-income home to a one-income home in a high-risk profession called journalism. This was a financial disaster, but I was convinced that I wanted to be home for my kid. That meant a few years of skimming hard on costs and comforts. No eating out or shopping or holidays. But gosh, the joy of bringing up a baby! She's now all grown up, and I look back with so much gratitude at my younger avatar for not letting me have regrets today. Those years are today worth all my net worth and more. They are priceless.

I was on a baby break for about seven years, and in those years I picked up odd writing jobs and editing projects, had signed up for the new emerging qualification called Certified Financial Planner (CFP), joined a training outfit and trained financial sector employees after a short course, and wrote for a US-based internet magazine (*Industry Standard*) during the Y2K boom years for which I got paid a dollar a word. That was the one year when we ate out, bought some decent clothes and took a holiday. And then the magazine shut down!

Anyhow, the short story is that I kept earning bits and pieces even while not formally working. I managed to requalify myself. And I learnt only to spend money after I earned it. I still remember buying my first AC in sweltering Delhi (we had moved back from Mumbai after a year) after getting paid for some editing work I did in 2001. But in all those tough money years, I still remember making at least some of that PPF contribution with dogged focus.

I found that if you look hard enough, you will find the money for things that are important to you. You need to decide what is important. So if you began reading this chapter thinking 'where is the money to invest', all I can tell you is that look harder, you'll find it. We all go through tough times.

Money is never in plenty in the early years. But getting into debt to fund current spending is not the way out. Either find a way to raise income or spend less. There is no third option. I did both. I requalified myself so that I could earn more and till then, I harshly cut spending. And I still managed to support the extended family financially despite the tight money squeeze. My only regret? I left investing in mutual funds for much later. I should have started earlier.

## Why we resist investing for the long-term

Not having money to invest is one of the four big reasons we put off the investing decision. At number two is the desire to keep money in a liquid form for a future emergency. Third is the fear of making a mistake, and fourth is the lack of knowledge. I shared my story here not to show off (well, maybe just a bit), but just to say that I've done what I'm asking you to do. It is possible. It is doable. And I have experimented with myself with all that I tell you. So what you get is fully cooked and not out of a textbook. Let's examine the four fears of investing.

## Show me the money

'Arrey, I'm not rich enough to start investing.' Not beginning the process of investing because you don't have a large corpus in the first place is like waiting to get fit before you join a diet and fitness routine. I will lay a part of the blame on the kind of media messaging that was prevalent till about fifteen years ago.

Investing in the stock market was seen as a gamble – the tip sheets gave you hot tips which would double your money overnight. The relentless coverage of the stock market minute by minute by the TV channels, the brokers talking about what's hot, and the breathless anchors who celebrated a rising Sensex, all made average salaried people think like traders and not investors. We all need to remember this: We are not stock market traders or speculators. There is a role for day traders and speculators in a stock market – but you and I are not traders. We are investors. Understand that difference.

A speculator must watch the market minute to minute, and periodically look at her mobile and exclaim a four-letter word. Or pump a fist with a Yesss! If you are doing any of that, you're reading the wrong book. This book is about investing and not stock market trading.

Look, we don't have large lump sums to invest. Most of us get a salary and out of that we save something every month. *We don't need a lot of money first to start investing*. We need a lot of little money streams to keep gathering to make a large corpus. Even if you begin with just Rs 1,000 a month, it is

Rs 12,000 more a year that you would have had a year ago. Most people admit to being able to save at least Rs 5,000–10,000 a month. And that's right after they tell me, 'Arrey, where is the money to invest?'

*The important thing to do is to start rather than wait for that golden moment when you have a big amount to hit the market with.* Your cash-flow system will tell you how much you can easily save each month. That's the amount you begin with. We'll talk about how much you can save and how much you need to save in the chapter on retirement.

## What if …

If you think about it, creating that emergency fund and buying all those insurance covers are a bit like using a seat belt. We don't know when an accident will happen, or what kind it will be, but the seat belt will prevent the unavoidable accidents from harming you to a certain extent.

Of course, if a giant truck wants to sniff the trunk of your car through the front windshield, there is nothing much you can do. But a seat belt does prevent the most preventable of injuries. Setting up of an emergency fund and buying insurance covers are ways to protect our money box from unavoidable events as you journey through life, and to reduce the damage to your finances they bring.

*But the financial seat belt does another thing – it reduces the need to keep most of your money ready at hand.* Keeping money ready to use for an emergency is one of the key reasons that people don't invest for the long term. But not just emergencies, we shy away from long-term investing for one more reason: What if I don't have the money to make the annual investment commitment? What if I change my mind? What if I find a better investment? What if this investment does not perform? What if they run away with my money – how can I trust some private company with my money? Worry two is about not having the money to invest or changing your mind about your long-term investment.

## I hate making mistakes

Have you heard the guy on the next sofa boasting about his stock market kill at a party? 'Bhaisaab, I told you to invest in that penny stock. I made a killing.' The group sips in a reverent silence. But ask him the question 'What is your portfolio return?', and you see the wind drop from the sails instantly. 'Who looks at portfolio return, medum? I look at my winning only, heh heh.'

The hits and misses tend to cancel out over the years when you 'punt' on a stock or on real estate. A lot of people do manage to invest, but find themselves in inefficient, high-cost, low-return products. A big reason why people stay in fixed deposits, gold, insurance and real estate is the fear of making errors.

We've grown up with FDs, land, insurance plans and gold as the holy grail of investment. Moving away from these into other financial products, such as mutual funds, means getting out of our comfort zone – and that is always scary. But remember this – it is better to have something in investments, even if it earns less, than not to have anything at all. *The purpose of this book is to migrate you from low-return, clunky products into financial products that look after the needs of a very different Indian citizen than of the 1970s' angry young man.*

## I'm a money dummy

'I don't know anything about investing.' Said with the right toss of the head and eye-roll, the dialogue conveys much more than the words. It says: Money is gross; I am too cool to spend my time thinking about it. It says: I have better things to do than do baniyagiri with profit and loss – leave that to the traders. What it actually means: I don't know anything about investing. I am so afraid of the future that I'm frozen.

This head toss and eye-roll is actually the defence mechanism to convince oneself that one has no option but to continue to live without a money plan. *What you need to remember is that understanding investing is a one-time fixed cost in terms of your time.* Once you get it, nobody can take it away from you. Once you get the logic of a financial plan and understand the basics, you can't get cheated again. It won't take long. You are a doctor, a lawyer, an engineer, a teacher, an entrepreneur, a homemaker – you are all smart people. You can do this. Remember that it is in the interest of the financial sector to make you believe that you are a money dummy. It just takes common sense and some time to 'get' finance.

Once you have talked yourself out of these fears, we can start the investing conversation. The cash-flow system already in place in your money box will help you see clearly what you can invest. We'll find out how much you need to save in the chapter on retirement. For now, let's just stay with the concept of investing and why we find it so difficult to do. Notice that we've begun to discuss investing in Chapter 6 and not Chapter 1.

We've been programmed to think about investment products by a commission-driven marketplace. How often has the person offering to solve your financial worries begun with 'So how much do you have to invest?' But the answer to how much to invest depends on so many things. It depends on why you want to invest, for how long you want to invest, how comfortable you are with taking a bit of risk to target a higher return.

It depends on how many people you have in your family; it depends on how secure your job is. It depends on what other products you have already in your money box. It depends on whether you are an entrepreneur, a salaried employee or a consultant.

It is almost an insult to be asked 'how much do you want to invest' before some of these questions are answered. The sales-push model of hawking the top-selling product of the month has harmed many people. *Remember that each financial product you buy must solve a problem you have.* It must have a purpose. Simply buying something because it is being hard-sold is just bad money-box behaviour. We don't do it here. Not cool.

I look at the investing decisions more as a cash-flow issue – will I have the money I need in the future, ready to use or not? The future could be next week, it could be three years later when I want to replace my dad's car, or it could be in ten years when I want to send my kid abroad. We worry about getting old but tuck it away till we can. Either look at the faces of your parents or grandparents and know that you will get there in time. Or download an app that ages your picture. Look at your own face when you are sixty. Then seventy, eighty. Ninety. Scary! And the scary part is that we will – most of us will – live to see ninety. Those in their early twenties can think of even longer lifespans.

## Onwards ho!

We are at the stage where we begin the process of filling our money boxes with investment products, and we must remember to find products that take care of some of these worries. The products we choose must justify their presence in the money box.

Pull out your mental money box and look at it again. Remember that the first cell has your cash flows, the second is the emergency fund, the third your medical cover, and the fourth has the life cover. We now create three more cells in the box for our investments. We name each cell: The first is called Almost-There; the second, In-Some-Time; and the third, Far-Away. Now there are seven cells.

## Now, then, when

Any planned expense that will happen within two to three years is a short-term need that you put down under Almost-There. Remember, I told you that you can use this money box to suit your own personality and financial situation. If you hate taking risk and are happier with lower efficiency, you can extend three years to four, or even five. But for most of us, a period of three years is the threshold of Almost-There in terms of financial needs. What could these needs be? Getting married, sending kid to school (some of these teaching shops take development fees that cost a bomb), buying a house, buying a car, going for a holiday, financing mum's surgery, buying dad a car – go on, you write a few down on that paper.

In-Some-Time are planned expenses that sit between three to seven years away. Already, it begins to get a bit difficult to plan ahead. But let's try. Depending on your age and stage, In-Some-Time could fill with down payment on your house, kids' higher-education fees, kids' marriage and your retirement. Write down what you think your unique In-Some-Time needs will be.

Far-Away are expenses that are really hard to imagine today. At age thirty to thirty-five it seems impossible that you will ever get old. I've crossed fifty, and even I find it difficult to think that I will fully retire, and will have to depend on my savings for living costs sometime in the not-so-distant future. And for you in your twenties and thirties, retirement must be truly that which happens to Martians. But look around you, at the faces of your grandparents (specially your grandmum) and parents, and understand fully that you will get there. You will. I will, we all will. The retirement question needs a full chapter to decode and we'll get there soon.

Next, we put down what each of these will cost you in the future. Put down a value next to each of these – what it costs today. For example, if you know that you will need money for a down payment on a house in two years, you know already what your budget is and approximately how much you will need in two years. But what if the goal is further away – say, you know that you want to send your kid abroad in six years for her undergraduate degree but she has no idea what she will do yet.

Though costs will vary across schools and cities, you will get a ballpark figure today. Put down your retirement as a goal for the Far-Away. There are very smart calculators that will do the numbers for you – of what you will need and how much you need to save today. The calculators will 'inflation-index' the present cost of your future goals.

This means that they will assume a rate of inflation and raise the cost of that goal, so you know approximately how much you will need in the future. Some calculators do more. They will also ask you to assume a certain rate of return, what you think you can earn on investments, and then come back and tell you what you need to save each year and month now to get to that goal. We'll discuss rates of return, inflation and products in the next few chapters.

This book is not about helping you with fixing exact numbers but about thinking about what products work in each of these boxes. Think of financial products like certain kinds of food. Take sugar – if taken in reasonable quantities, sugar-filled foods are fine for a person who is healthy, but is poison for a diabetic. Or take salt – works just fine for most people; but have hypertension, and salt is gunpowder. Financial products are similar. Not everything suits everybody – *we need to match our financial needs to financial products*.

Hmmm, you say: This looks like the end of this book. No way we can match six billion people to products in a book. Luckily, there is a way to work this out. We match products to your holding period. Or look at it this way: Each financial product has a certain time period over which it works best. A product that is very safe in the long run becomes very risky in the short term. And a product that works in the short term becomes a drag on returns if you hold it too long. When you now think of a financial product, learn to ask the question: Over what holding time period does this work the best?

Before we start talking about products to put into the cells, we need to understand what is out there. You know the pitches from insurance companies and mutual funds; you know the doubling-money stories from people who bought the right share at the right time. You hear with envy the stories of Rs 5 lakhs becoming 5 crores through property. But you never seem to buy the right product. Everybody says this:

I am the unluckiest person ever born. I just have to invest in the market, and it crashes.

Listen to this. Even if you were the unluckiest investor in the world and bought into the market on the worst day possible, there is a way in which you can still win. But to get to that point, we need a short ride in the 'Asset Car'. More about that in the next chapter.

> It is never the 'right' time to begin investing. You feel you are too poor or too young or too dumb to begin. The right time is now. No matter what your age, stage or circumstance is, you need to begin investing right away. But investing according to a plan.
> 
> **You are doing okay if**
> 
> 1. you are committed to drawing up an investment plan;
> 2. you have written down your near-, medium- and long-term goals;
> 3. you have put a monetary value to these goals; and
> 4. you understand what amount you need to invest today.

# FINALLY, WE'RE INVESTING

Why do we run away from LONG-TERM INVESTMENTS?

- What if I make a mistake?
- What if I fail to meet my annual investment commitment?
- I don't understand investments!

## STRUCTURING YOUR MONEY BOX

↓ ↓ ↓

Your inflows, outflows & surplus, ie. your financial life, in a box!

Emergency Funds & Insurance Cover

**BANKS, FDs** — A FINANCIAL SAFETY CUSHION REDUCES THE NEED TO KEEP MOST OF YOUR MONEY READY AT HAND!

| CASH FLOWS | | | EMERGENCY FUND | MEDICAL COVER | LIFE COVER |
|---|---|---|---|---|---|
| INCOME | SPEND-IT | INVESTMENT | | | |

### ALMOST-THERE
**SHORT-TERM NEEDS:** Planned expenses within 3 years.
e.g., buying car, kids' school, holiday, getting married, mum's surgery

### IN-SOME-TIME
Planned expenses that are 3-7 years away.
e.g., down payment of a house, kids' education or marriage

### FAR-AWAY
Predicted expenses that are farther away into the future.
e.g., retirement, world tour

## NOT EVERYTHING SUITS EVERYBODY!

We need to match our financial needs to financial products.

# 7

# LET'S DE-JARGON INVESTING

*We are too fond of our gold, real estate and FDs. Let's understand the true nature of each of these investments and what purpose they serve in our money box.*

There was a time a few years back when my (then) teenager was sick of me. Nothing new in the history of teenage issues with parents, but she had (still has) a unique problem. It is not the usual teenage 'how-dumb-can-you-be' gripe or the 'will-you-just-get-off-my-case' grunt, or even 'how-did-you-get-so-far-with-so-little-brain' eye-roll. No. It's a totally new one that will put books on managing teenagers off track.

She's fed up of me 'talking money' wherever I go. Any amount of telling her that I do not initiate such conversations cuts no ice. Things got dangerous when the hair-cutting lady began discussing her financial life. While my daughter made retching, gagging noises, I tried to hear what the lady with the scissors said over the whine of the hairdryer. I learnt my lesson from Calvin (brother to Hobbes), who advises that it is always good to be nice to the person who holds something sharp near your neck. So I chose to answer hairdresser questions and dealt with the mutant teenager later.

The hair-cutting lady's worries were about not doing anything much with her money – the nagging feeling that she was standing still while everybody else was zipping past on fantastic money moves. She ended with a statement that I hear all the time: 'Anyway I don't understand all this stuff. Goes over my head. I see numbers and my eyes glaze. I'm too stupid to understand finance.' She, by the way, is smart enough to raise kids as a single mom, look after her old mother and run a small parlour all on her own. Not stupid at all.

You keep hearing the suits on TV talk about asset classes, portfolios, underlying,* deficit and interest rate corridors, and get really intimidated. Get this straight. It is in the interest of the financial sector to keep things tough for you. The less you understand, the more you can be cheated. The more complicated you think the world is, the more they can obfuscate. But I just said, earlier in the book, that you need a financial planner because of the large number of choices and

---

* The suits use 'underlying' all the time to confuse people; all it means is the product in which the investment is made. So in an equity mutual fund, the underlying is stocks.

decisions. Well, I'm saying both. Basic finance is not tough to understand, choosing products is. But if you understand basics, you can ask the right questions of the person selling you a product or even of your financial planner. There is a way to do it yourself fully, and I discuss that in the chapter on products just ahead.

I'm going to give you a quick update on the different kinds of financial products in the market and which bucket of 'asset class' they belong to. Think of it this way: If you had four boxes and had to sort a bunch of fruit, what would you do? You'd put the papaya in the papaya box. The jamun would go in the jamun box, mangoes with other mangoes, and oranges with their brothers and sisters. While we call them all fruit, they are all different. They taste different, and are good for some people and not so good for others. A diabetic is advised to eat less mangoes and more jamun. An arthritic less orange and more papaya. You have to find the fruit that suits your health and taste needs rather than buy what your neighbour is buying.

Financial products are no different. *There is a purpose for each product you buy, and each product needs to fight with others to grab that place in your box.* There are three asset classes that we need to understand. Debt, equity and real assets.

Debt is just an umbrella term for all financial products that are based on borrowing. Equity is ownership of a business and the risk that it brings, either directly (through stocks) or indirectly (through mutual funds). Real assets are those that can be physically seen. Debt and equity are called 'financial assets', while real estate and gold are called 'real assets'. Each of these three buckets has certain features and you need parts of all three in your money box.

## Debt

Let's start with what we understand really well. We are already investing in the category called 'debt'. We may not call it that. The word 'debt' makes us think of the debts that we have – car loans, home loans and credit card loans. But when used by the sharp *Suits*, debt means the cell with products that give you an assured return – like a bank fixed deposit or a tax-free bond or a public provident fund.

The core of the product is a loan. When you make a deposit with the bank, it treats it as a loan from you. And needs to give a periodic return, and then the principal back to you after an agreed-upon time. These are products where two things are fixed – how much you will get back and when you will get it back. You are loaning money to the bank or the bond issuer and the interest is the *price* of this loan.

Why do you get an interest on your money? Because by not using it today, you have postponed consumption – you need to be compensated for that. By pushing the use of Rs 1 lakh to five years later, you take the risk of the money losing value to inflation – you must be compensated for that. By lending money, you also take the risk of the borrower not returning it – you need to be compensated for that.

Ever wondered why government bonds pay the lowest interest? Because they are the safest. That is why a real-estate company will have to offer interest rates on its corporate deposits much higher than a bank FD to get your money. They are offering a higher interest as a sweetener for the higher risk you take. You must remember this each time you are offered a company deposit or a 'scheme' that offers you very high interest rates. The higher the return it promises, the higher is the risk – even in a product you think is 'safe' like a company deposit.

Think of your bank FD rate as your benchmark or measuring rod. Better get used to this term – you will hear a lot of it. A benchmark is a standard you measure something against. Remember the time when a first division in school was a big deal. Today a score of 90 per cent or above has the same status. The benchmark for good performance thirty years ago was 60 per cent or above; today that benchmark has moved up.

Without a benchmark there is no comparison of returns in finance. If somebody offers you a rate of interest that is much higher than a bank FD, understand that the risk of non-payment of both your investment and the interest on this deal is much higher.

We will include your provident fund, public provident fund, fixed deposits, corporate deposits, all the small savings products, bonds of all kinds under the heading of 'debt'. Some of these products come with tax benefits and some do not. A simple internet search will show you the tax treatment of each of these products. There is another category of 'debt' products that carries more risk than the guaranteed-return products mentioned above. These are debt mutual funds. Let's deal with these just a bit later, in the mutual fund chapter.

*The role of debt products in your money box is to provide money at short notice and to provide stability to your long-term investments.* Debt products need to give you a degree of certainty that the money will be there when you want it. This is unlike equity which is much more volatile – prices go up and down almost on a daily basis. They also make up the core of your long-term investments. For example, your EPF (employees' provident fund) and PPF (public provident fund) are the core of your retirement corpus. These are safe, tax-free, and provide that rock-solid core to your portfolio.

Why not put all your money into debt products? After all we want to be certain about what we get back in the future?

We don't put all our long-term money into debt because we want the growth that equity can give to our money. Debt products are good for stability but not for growth.

## Gold

We think we understand gold and real estate quite well, but we don't, at least not as well as we think we do. Let's talk about gold. Indians are accused of hoarding gold – having a gold fixation – causing India's import bill to rise. It is true; as a country we hold a lot of gold, and most of it is with the households. But, I think it is unfair to blame us for our gold fixation. The fault sits firmly with the government and regulators that have not cleaned up the game in the retail financial products market.

We don't trust the products or the people selling them. We find that our money in the bank is eroded by inflation. Inflation is most often a result of bad government policy. To mitigate the risk of fraud and inflation, we have traditionally bought gold. The government calling us stupid is double the insult.

Other than a vote of no confidence in the financial sector, is there a need to hold gold? What is the role of gold, why should it occupy a place in our money box at all? Ideally, gold is good as a hedge against inflation. This means that the price of gold rises over the years, so that your money does not lose purchasing power. Gold does not give an interest like your bank deposit. It does not throw off dividend like a stock. Nor does it give rent, like your property. The only way you can profit from gold is when its value goes up – when you actually make a profit. So, how good is gold for getting capital gains or profits?

The answer is it depends when you bought it and how long you held it. If you bought when gold prices were down, you made a large profit. If you bought gold when prices were high, you made a loss. If you held gold long enough, your returns kept your purchasing power intact – you got a positive real return.

Remember these are bullion prices. If you bought jewellery thinking you are making an investment, you have not counted all the costs properly. You lose 30 per cent straightaway to making charges when you buy gold as jewellery. No, I'm not saying no to jewellery. I enjoy my own gold trinkets, but I'm sure that these are not part of my investments at all. I buy jewellery because I enjoy wearing or gifting it. For my investments, I stay with mutual funds.

But the funds discussion needs to wait. We need to understand that every investment we make has costs – some we can see, others we cannot or prefer not to – like the making charges for gold jewellery. When you go to sell your gold jewellery, you lose another 10 to 30 per cent depending on the purity of gold and making charges. Few people actually sell gold jewellery to bring home the profit; it is usually gifted one generation to the next. So buying gold jewellery as investment just does not make sense. There are other ways to hold gold.

Given the role of gold in our families and the need to gift gold at weddings in India, do buy gold. But buy it sensibly. *Not more than 5–10 per cent of your total portfolio goes into gold. You do not buy jewellery as investment.* Your options to buy gold are coins, bars, gold exchange-traded funds (ETFs) and gold bonds from the government. From 2017, the smart investment decision is to buy the bonds issued by the Government of India; these bonds give you not only the full market value of gold when you sell the bonds in the future, but also a small interest on your investment each year. All other ways of holding gold have a cost attached to them and do not give a regular return. I'm ignoring all the tax-not-paid cash that goes into gold. We're only dealing with legit money.

## Real estate

After gold, our next obsession is real estate. Like gold, Indians think they have a special relationship with real estate. Real estate is a sure thing in the minds of most people with investing on their minds. A friend's brother is a senior executive in a public sector firm in Jaipur. He has his own inherited house in a good neighbourhood and is looking ahead to a good pension in some years.

But in 2014, he made a strange investment. He bought a flat in one of the Gurgaon high-rises. He took a fifteen-year loan that soaked up almost 40 per cent of his post-tax income. He mortgaged his Jaipur house, because he was so close to retirement that the bank needed collateral. He signed on to pay a hefty Rs 15,000 a month as maintenance charges.

My friend asked me to talk some sense into her brother. I did. I remember talking to him just before he made the investment. Why are you doing this? You have your home already. You will retire before the home loan is paid off. You don't have black money. Real estate is a terrible investment at current price levels. It is better to put this EMI money in an equity mutual fund or even your provident fund rather than a depreciating asset. But bhai was all set.

His friend circle had stories to tell of money multiplied in real-estate deals. He felt as if he were being left behind. His wife too kept pushing him on – we're not doing anything, everybody else is getting rich, I should have married the businessman my dad had proposed instead of 'salary class'... Anyway, ye mutual fund-shund toh amiron ka khel hai, sab ghotala hai. And that led to a rant about the stock market and Harshad Mehta and the scams since. The conversation ends.

I usually exit a conversation when it falls to an illogical, emotional rant about unrelated issues. We forget how many of our money decisions are related to emotions, power equations within the family and suppressed issues that tend to erupt at some random trigger. So I said, whatever, not my money. Bhai goes and books the flat a week later.

Then in 2018, the flat began sucking up a chunk of his salary. He'd spent another Rs 10 lakhs to do it up – state-of-the art kitchen with German hobs, Italian marble. As an aside: think about it – why would you pay for stone to be quarried in another country and shipped to become your kitchen slab when there is perfectly good stone available locally? Did it have to do with the salesman saying with a curl of the lip – we only deal in imported marble; for the Indian stuff you need to go elsewhere.

So much of our buying decisions has to do with what other people think of us. And that Rs 15,000 maintenance is just the additional expense that is slowly strangling the household budget. The rent he gets is not even half the EMI.

Bhai now begins to panic, retirement is just round the corner, and the 'always-up' real-estate market has gone into a funk. He thinks of selling. The market is flat and he's getting just about what he paid for it. Chalo, at least investment to wapas aa gaye, he told me. But what about the interest cost of the loan you took, I twist the knife. Add the ten lakhs of doing-up cost, the monthly maintenance bill, and deduct the rent from the costs, and he is staring at a loss. Chalo ji, long term mein sab theek ho jayega.

He's now holding on till he makes a small profit on his investment. And all the while he's hurtling towards retirement, funnelling money in an asset that will take a long, long time to recover. He could have been funnelling it into a hybrid mutual fund that would have given a return of at least 9–10 per cent a year, post cost.

But that's the real-estate story. *It is a horrible, clunky, chunky investment that has lots of costs, which people forget to add to the profit maths.* It is illiquid – you can't sell in a hurry. You can't sell one room to raise some funds – you need to sell the whole darn property. It needs periodic investments for maintenance. For society flats, there is the added cost of high charges. But we remain wedded to real estate.

Why do we like it so much? There are three reasons why people can't think beyond real estate. Habit, black money and fear. We've grown up thinking of real estate as a long-term investment.

We've grown up on nani–dadi stories about how their haveli or land in the village that cost just a few thousand rupees is now valued at crores. '*Agar usko tab becha na hota to aaj ye din na ...*' is a common conversation thread in many families. The reason people think real estate is a great investment is that they look at the return in absolute terms, from point to point. The flat that sold for Rs 1 crore was bought for just ten lakhs, is something we've heard so often.

Lost in this conversation is the fact that the distance between the buying and selling price is twenty-seven years, costs of maintenance, property taxes, brokerage and insurance. The effective return rate, before any of these costs, is 9 per cent a year.

Doesn't look that great any more, does it? Moneywise people will break this habit of thinking that real estate is sure-shot money and that you can't go wrong with it. Lots of horrible things can happen – the title can be disputed, the land or flat can get grabbed, the tenant may refuse to get out ... When I think of the risk associated with real estate, I seriously wonder what people see in it.

And that brings me to my second reason for our love for real estate – black money. Gold and real estate have been the sumps of black money in India. Most of the second sales in real estate take place in cash, and dealing in black is like a treadmill – once you get on it, you have to keep running with the money. The habit of black money is so strong that we cannot even imagine a situation where a cash component is the exception and a full cheque payment is the norm.

I remember when my husband and I were in the market for a house, we had to pay a price for making a full cheque payment. After seeing at least twenty properties, we realized that we'll never buy – about 60–70 per cent of the payment had to be in cash. Our choice set finally reduced to one old man who had the same moral fibre as ours and wanted a full cheque.

So unless you have illegal money (basically money on which you have not paid tax), stay well away from real estate as investment in India – the prices are inflated due to cash in the system, and residential yields remain very low.

The third reason to choose real estate is just fear of the unknown. Twenty to thirty years ago, there were not many investment avenues – gold, real estate, bank deposits and LIC were what everybody had chosen to invest in. But now the presence of mutual funds, which have a product for most needs, does give a better choice set. But these are invisible products – we can neither see them, live in them, nor wear them. They do not come with government guarantees. This makes us fearful. The stock market scams of the past haunt us, as they should.

We should be very careful where we invest our money. We're happy to invest in dodgy property deals, to risk builders running away with our money and to turn our white into black so that we can invest for the long term in something we are familiar with and can 'trust'. Time for pressing reset.

The Indian habit of gold, FD and real estate is hard to break. But why buy the '60s and '70s products when you have the millennial financial products to invest in. Count the costs, count in the years of investing and look at post-tax returns to see the true face of your investment returns.

**You are doing okay if**

1. you have no more than 5 to 10 per cent of your portfolio in gold and they are in the form of government gold bonds;
2. you own one house as the roof over your head, and no more;
3. you have your FDs, PF and PPF, debt funds and no other debt products, no corporate deposits, no chit funds, no AT1 bonds; and
4. your debt allocation is equal to your age; at age thirty, no more than 30 per cent of your portfolio is in debt products; at age seventy, no more than 70 per cent in debt products; the rest is equity.

# LET'S DE-JARGON INVESTING

When investing, we need to understand 3 asset classes: DEBT, EQUITY and REAL ASSETS

FINANCIAL ASSET → EQUITY / DEBT PRODUCTS

REAL ASSETS → GOLD / REAL ESTATE

## GOLD

COINS, BARS, GOLD EXCHANGE TRADE FUNDS & GOLD BONDS ARE INVESTMENTS!

NOT MORE THAN 5-10% OF TOTAL PORTFOLIO GOES INTO GOLD

jewellery is not an investment!
- 30% in making charges
- 20% on purity of gold

## DEBT PRODUCTS

- products that give you an assured return.

e.g., bank fixed deposit, bonds, public provident fund.

Bank treats this as a loan from you and gives you periodic returns & the principal back after an agreed-upon time.

## REAL ESTATE

Actual cost:
- Buying price
- + property tax
- + brokerage
- + maintenance
- Selling price

Post all costs, EFFECTIVE RETURNS are LOWER than we believe.

MONEY DECISIONS — EMOTIONS

Agar is zameen ko tab becha nahi hota toh aaj iski keemat...

**LOW** — RISK RETURNS

PROVIDE MONEY AT SHORT NOTICE

Debt allocation must be equal to your age!

# 8

# EQUITY

*The most misunderstood of all asset classes, stocks are not a lottery where some people get lucky. There is a math and science, and a way to take risk safely.*

This is my favourite asset class but I don't buy shares directly. It is really important to understand the difference between investing in stocks directly and getting an equity exposure. The toughest learning is the one around equity, as it is misunderstood to be a gamble rather than a slow builder of wealth. **Equity is a slow cook and not instant noodles.**

To understand equity, we need to understand how a business works. There are two ways by which entrepreneurs can fund their businesses – debt and equity. Imagine that your friend makes the best biryani in Delhi. But she makes it at home for her friends and family. You and others egg her on and she sets up a small home takeaway service. The biryani delivery is a runaway hit. She wants to expand the business – she wants to set up five kitchens in different parts of the city and grow the business fivefold.

Now she will have to rent the kitchen premises, hire more people and get more equipment. The cost of this expansion is Rs 30 lakhs. She can borrow the money from a bank, but you and a few more friends decide to stake her out. Four of you contribute Rs 5 lakhs each; she puts in another Rs 10 lakhs. On a pro-rata basis, each of you now owns a slice of the biryani business; she owns twice your one-sixth share. You four have one share each and she has two shares in the business.

The business does well. At the end of the year the profit is Rs 12 lakhs. Each 'share' in the business makes a profit of Rs 2 lakhs. You decide not to take home the profit, but invest it further in the business.

From the Rs 12 lakh profit, she opens even more kitchens. The profit in year two is Rs 20 lakhs.

One friend is going abroad and wants to sell his 'share'. He had paid Rs 5 lakhs for his share and is now willing to sell. Will he sell for Rs 5 lakhs or more? More, right? Because the company is profitable and has gathered value; the price at which he will sell will be more than Rs 5 lakhs. If you want to buy his share, you will look at what potential this biryani business has to earn profits and then you will make an offer.

You will do the maths and may be willing to pay Rs 15 lakhs. This Rs 10 lakhs he has made is his 'profit'. He had invested Rs 5 lakhs and he is selling his share at

Rs 15 lakhs. This is what 'capital appreciation' means in the language of the stock market.

Shares gather value not because of some magic wand, but because there is value ahead for the buyer of the stock. If there is value, why does the guy sell? For many reasons – the stock price may have hit a number the seller targeted, he may need the money, he may not see the value.

Now she wants to expand even more. Her daughter has just finished an MBA and wants to transform this kitchen business into a corporate multi-city chain. They now need Rs 10 crores to do this. How to raise this money? Again, they can go to the bank or they can 'list' this company.

That means they can sell shares of the biryani company to anybody who sees value in it and wants to be a part of its business. Each of the original shares that had a value of Rs 5 lakhs will now be broken down into many 'shares' – each with a 'face value' of Rs 10.

But when they sell their shares to the public, they sell not at the 'face value' or the original value of the share, but at a 'premium'. The profit-making business now will sell at a premium and not at Rs 10 per share. What this premium will be is decided by looking at the future prospects of this business, the management expertise, the competition in the market and many other factors.

How to find the people who want to invest? Firms that want to raise 'equity' capital go to a stock exchange. This is a marketplace where firms get themselves listed. This means the stock exchange has some basic rules of hygiene that the firm must stick to.

Think of a local market that is run by the municipal authority. The rules are that each shop must have a registration number, must maintain some cleanliness, must obey the market-closing time, must provide an hour of lunch break for employees, and so on. Only shopkeepers that stick to rules can open a store. A stock market also has some rules that firms that want to be listed must obey.

I will not get into a detailed study of these rules because we don't need to know them at this stage. But what you need to remember is that as markets grow and events happen, these rules of the game also change. A stock exchange has an oversight authority called the capital market regulator. In India, this entity is called the Securities and Exchange Board of India (SEBI).

SEBI sets up the rules of the game around the equity market. Stock exchanges have to abide by them. The firms that list have to abide by SEBI and stock exchange rules. *What you need to understand is that when we talk about investing in equity, we are not talking about gambling on the street.* This is a legitimate marketplace with rules.

Retail investors who make big losses on the stock market are people who don't follow the rules that small investors must follow. Remember, there are professionals whose day job is to decode firms and markets. If you — a part-time, occasional investor — think you can outsmart them, you are either very lucky or delusional.

# EQUITY

IS NOT A GAMBLE, IT'S MATHS & SCIENCE & CALCULATED RISK

**STOCK EXCHANGE** is a marketplace where firms that want to raise money from investors get themselves LISTED.

**SEBI:** Securities and Exchange Board of India. It is the oversight authority that sets up the RULES around CAPITAL MARKETS.

An **INDEX** is made up of companies that represent the sectors they operate in. SENSEX and NIFTY 50 are broad market or large-cap indices. There are many such indices like mid-cap index, small-cap index, and BankEx to name a few.

**SENSEX & NIFTY 50** are a barometer of the activity on a stock market over short & long periods of time. Sensex has 30 most representative stocks & Nifty50 has 50.

## HOW DOES ALL THIS WORK?

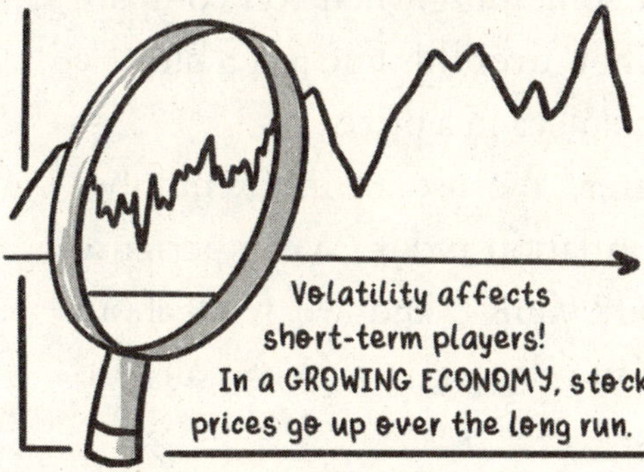

Volatility affects short-term players! In a GROWING ECONOMY, stock prices go up over the long run.

### HOW?
→ Legitimate firms get listed
→ Firms grow in a growing economy
→ Profits → better return to shareholders

## What is the Sensex?

You need to be living under a rock deep in the Bay of Bengal to have escaped meeting Mr Sensex. He is Amitabh Bachchan and Shah Rukh Khan rolled into one for the business channels. His movements are closely tracked. When he is exuberantly happy, TV anchors put on party caps and cut cakes. When he throws a major tantrum by crashing down, they look as if somebody died. If a government that the 'market' does not like comes to power, Mr Sensex makes his blue mood clear by falling like a stone in water. When the government announces more economic reform, such as the GST (goods and services tax), he throws a party by touching a 'lifetime high'. Who's this Mr Sensex and why should we worry about his up-and-down moods?

Well, as long-term investors, my suggestion is to ignore Mr Sensex. But before you do that, understand who he is, why he is irrelevant to your life in the short term, but very important in the long run. To understand Mr Sensex better, we need to understand a stock market index, because that's what he is. What is an index number? It is a number that shows the change in price of something when you compare it with its price in the past. Chew over this line just a bit. We are using a number to track changes in a price.

Let's understand this better. We use an index number all the time and that is the inflation index. We experience inflation when we go to buy things, and we read about inflation when the government releases data. We've all read that inflation is up or down, but what does that mean? It means that the index number — the consumer price index — that tracks consumer inflation is going up or down as compared to the previous number.

What is the inflation index made up of? Does it comprise all the goods and services in the country? That would be an impossible task, so the index is made up of the most representative items, such as food, fuel, clothing, housing, among others. The big spends for the consumers are included as representative of all the expenses. Each of these further breaks down into its most representative items.

For example, food will further include cereals, eggs, meat, fruits, vegetables, milk and beverages. Each of these categories will get further broken down into its most representative items. For instance, there are over thirty varieties of mango in India, but the index will only include a few based on how popular a type of mango is and how large its share is in the total sales of mangoes in the country. Yes, I'm sure *haphus* is there in the index.

With me so far? OK, now, the prices of some items in the index will go up and the prices of some things will go down. For example, the price of a telephone call has fallen sharply over the last ten years, but the price of dal has more than tripled. Ups and downs in price will cancel each other out, but if price rises on the average have been more than the price falls, the index will rise — and we will say inflation is rising. If the opposite happens, we get data to say inflation is falling.

Our individual experience of buying something in the market may not reflect the broad trend of inflation. For example, you go to buy milk and find the prices have gone up. But the index may be down because the price fall in fuel and several other things have cancelled out the price rise in milk.

We can use this understanding of the price index to now meet Mr Sensex. The Sensex is made up of thirty most representative companies that are listed on the Bombay Stock Exchange (BSE). The index has an initial value of 100, as on 1 April 1979.

The index is made up of companies that represent the sectors they operate in. They are also companies that are most traded on the stock market. When we say the Sensex went up, we mean that of the thirty companies in the Sensex more prices rose than fell.

The opposite is true when the Sensex falls. The Sensex is the barometer of the activity on a stock market during the day, and over a long period of time. So when you hear the words 'the Sensex is up', it does not mean that somebody threw down dice and the market went up. It just means that more prices went up than down for thirty companies!

The Nifty50 is another index that tracks the market health. This is made up of fifty stocks. India has two large exchanges – the BSE and the NSE – and both will have their own set of indices.

The Sensex and Nifty50 are broad market indices and are also called large-cap indices. You must have heard the term 'market cap' or 'market capitalization' – this is just the number of shares of the company multiplied by the price. If the firm has 100 shares in the market and they currently sell at Rs 50 per share, then the market cap is Rs 5,000.

Actually the number of shares runs into lakhs, and the price can be in triple digits, so the market-cap numbers look much bigger than our example. India's largest company by market cap is Reliance Industries Ltd with a market cap of over Rs 19 lakh crores as of August 2024. The 30th company's market cap is almost Rs 3 lakh crores. The 100th company on the BSE has just over almost Rs 97,000 crores of market cap.

To be included in the thirty-stock Sensex, the listed company needs to have a pretty large capitalization. This means that they have plenty of shares in the market and the price level is not in single digits either.

Large market-cap companies are usually the mature, established firms in the market. They are known for giving dividends rather than rapid growth. SEBI defines a large-cap company as one that features within the first 100 companies by market cap on the stock market. A mid-cap is a company that ranks between 101 to 250 by market cap, and small-caps are 251 and below.

Do the Sensex companies change or do they remain the same over time? Just as new products and services enter the consumer price index and old ones become less important, so also the sectors and firms within the Sensex change. The Sensex was formally launched on 2 January 1986 with thirty most actively traded stocks of that period, with 1 April 1979 as the base year, and an initial value of 100.

In 1986, the Sensex was made up of companies that included ACC, Bombay Dyeing, Great Eastern Shipping, Gwalior Rayon, Mukund and Zenith. These exited the index by 2004, and today there is a new set of companies with just five of the original thirty still in the Sensex. Mr Sensex throws out the companies that are no longer the largest and bestselling, and includes companies that represent the new areas of activity in the country. Gone are the cement, steel, commodity and engineering stocks. The changing face of Mr Sensex reflects the market change from the 1980s to date.

For example, banking, telecom and pharma were sectors that did not find a place in the 1980s Sensex, but are now firmly in the index. Companies are included and excluded based on a formula and not because the company chairman is friends with the SEBI chairman or the CEO of the stock exchange.

If you could just buy the Sensex or Nifty50, you would hold automatically the large, bestselling companies in India that represent the sectors of the economy that are doing well. Jump to the next chapter if you want to know how to do this right away.

## What is a mid-cap index? And is the BankEx also an index?

Suppose you wanted to track just food inflation and not the overall inflation in all consumer goods. You would create another index that would look at prices of just the items that are included under food. Then, within food, if you wanted to track inflation in vegetables and fruit? Yup, right, you then use the vegetable and fruit index. Use the same logic to understand the stock market.

The Sensex and Nifty50 are broad market indicators to the price change on a stock exchange, just as the consumer price index is the broad barometer of price changes that affect Indian consumers. The mid-cap index tracks only the representative mid-cap companies. These are companies that are smaller in size than the big, mature companies that sit in the Sensex. Being smaller, they have lower market cap and fewer shares out for trade. Their growth and fall both can be sharp.

A small-cap index will track firms that are even smaller. A BankEx will track the stocks of the banking sector. A PSU index will track the prices of just PSUs (public sector undertakings). A technology index will map the prices of tech firms. An infra index will track prices of infrastructure-related stocks. A FMCG index will track just the prices of FMCG (fast-moving consumer goods) firms. If you can think of an idea, you can create an index around it.

*Just as a food index will be more volatile (prices will go up and down with greater intensity) than a broader consumer price index, so also the Sensex will be more stable than the changes in a mid-cap index or a sector index.* Volatility affects those who deal in the stock market for short periods of time, but the longer you allow an index to work, the lower the effect of volatility.

In a growing economy, stock prices go up over the long run. Why's that? Think about it. The stock market in not a casino; it is a place where legitimate firms list so that the public and institutions can take part in its business through buying shares in businesses. Firms make goods and provide services. As they grow, their profits rise. Good profits and potential growth are the basis for stock price rise. Rising prices, over the long term, reflect the growth and profits of a company.

Why do I say that stocks are the best route to get inflation-adjusted returns? Or returns that are higher than the rise in prices. Remember that FD returns usually get you returns that destroy your purchasing power. What is it about stock prices that make it inflation-adjusted? Again, go back to basics. As inflation rises in the system, the input costs for the firms go up – they are passed on to the consumers in the form of higher final prices. The 'margins' or the profits of the firm, therefore, get protection from the effect of input price inflation.

## Why do I like giving my money an equity exposure so much?

Each time I show one slide in my workshops, lectures and talks, the audience gasps. There is disbelief on the faces at what they see. What is this slide? It shows the value of Rs 1 lakh invested in 1990 today in four different products. One, a fixed deposit. Two, gold. Three, public provident fund. Four, Sensex. Rs 1 lakh invested in each of these products and left to compound is worth around Rs 20 lakhs in the FD, gold and PPF, but the Rs 1 lakh invested in the Sensex is now more than Rs 85 lakhs.

How did this happen? Surely gold did better? If you understood the first part of this chapter, and the book till now, you will understand these numbers too. FDs are low-return investments that destroy purchasing power due to the impact of inflation. PPF does better because of higher rates of interest. Gold does badly because its price goes through highs and lows, and while there are periods in the history of gold that could have made you a lot of money, over time it does not beat equity index returns.

What is the magic about the Sensex that over thirty-four years the money has grown exponentially? There is no magic. In a growing economy, a broad market index will always have the well-performing stocks of that time. Any investment that allows you to buy the index stocks in the same proportion will give you index returns. You also get the benefit of the dividends declared and the bonus shares issued as you hold the index. Therefore the super returns over time.

Long ago when I was editing *Outlook Money*, I set out to do one exercise. We were used to taking point-to-point returns of the Sensex – that is, we pick a date and see what the return was one year back, two years back, ten years back, twenty years back and so on. But what if the date we pick is a day when the market is really high? Will we not get inflated returns? What if it is the lowest in the year?

I wanted to track an investment in the Sensex on a given day in a year in the past thirty years across various time periods. Suppose you invested Rs 1 lakh in the Sensex on 1 January 1980 and then held that investment for one year. You did the same on 2 January 1980 and held that for one year. Then you bought on 3 January and held for one year ... and you went on doing this for thirty years. There were days when you bought when the market was very low and your money more than doubled in a year. There were days on which you bought very high and your money halved in a year.

Now do the same exercise with a holding period of two years. You buy on 1 January 1980 and hold for two years. You buy on 2 January and hold for two years ... you do this across thirty years. Your maximum return and maximum loss are now lower than your previous experience. Do this exercise for a five-year holding period. Then ten, then twelve, thirteen, and so on.

Around year seven, you begin to get a very interesting result: the volatility of returns begins to reduce and the average return is about 14–15 per cent a year. Depending on a number of factors, the year at which the minimum return is positive is between seven and ten years. I finally had evidence on long-term investing!

I remember starting the process at about 2 p.m. in the afternoon. Next when I looked up, it was dark outside. It was extensive figure work, but the amazing results made me even more determined to bring equity exposure to middle-class India's money and end its dependency on gold, real estate and FDs.

You've heard this phrase so often – it is not market timing but time in the market that matters. *Time in the market matters because it smoothens out the volatility of the market.* Which is why you should not put money into the equity market if you need it next year.

## Equity vs real estate

Ask any group of people what gives the highest return, and nine out of ten will say real estate. The tenth will name gold as the best investment. Mention stocks or equity, and the response is either hostile, due to the stock-market–related scams (including the unpunished scam of unit-linked insurance plans), or fearful.

Every time I speak to a group, I get the same response: a sure thing with real estate and gold, and an overall feeling of mistrust with equity. Let's unpack this a bit. Let's look at return rates. I will do this in two parts.

One, historical returns. If we begin with the Sensex in June 1980 at 127.9 (Sensex was at 100 on 1 April 1979) as a starting point for a meaningful comparison, and look at returns across the market, real estate and gold, we get a positive return for all three.

Investment in gold, as we saw above, has been positive in the long term, but went into negative territory for a few years if the investment was made at one gold peak in 2012.

Investment in the Sensex returned around 16 per cent per year over the same period, that is, between 1979 and 2020.

Tracking real estate is tougher due to lack of data and location issues. So I picked the village where buffaloes bathed earlier but which has turned to a boomtown now, i.e., Gurgaon, to see what the price change has been for one of the best locations. Speaking to original inhabitants from the 1980s of what is now DLF City, I get rough rates of an investment of Rs 2 lakhs turning into Rs 2 crores over thirty-four years, or an average annual growth rate of 15 per cent. In fact, the thirty-year return ending 2021-22 on real estate is around 9 per cent.

But remember, both gold and real estate have high transaction costs that equity does not have. The returns in hand in both cases will be lower than with equity.

Two, now let's look at slice-of-time returns because this broad-sweep data hides individual stories of an investor buying an Infosys and another buying Satyam. It hides the stories of an investor buying in Gurgaon and another in Faridabad. The broad-sweep data will not talk to anybody who was in the market to buy a flat between 2003 and 2008 and lived through one of the biggest price reratings of urban housing in India.

I remember I was, and the price of the flat that cost Rs 30 lakhs in the beginning of 2003 kept rising every few weeks. Finally, it settled at about Rs 2 crores by late 2008 – a breathtaking 46 per cent compounded annual growth rate over five years. And there was a year in which prices doubled in Delhi real estate. But this is exactly the same as timing the equity market.

Those who bought real estate between 2003 and 2006 got lucky (and it really wasn't that they knew that Alan Greenspan was keeping rates low and flooding the world with cheap money!). As did equity investors over that period. Sensex returns over 2003 to 2008 stand at around 35 per cent a year. Again there was a year from mid-2009 to 2010 when the market doubled! Both real estate and the Sensex returned 20 per cent a year from 2003 to 2014.

Remember these numbers do not take into account transaction costs, taxes, cost of maintenance of the investment or inflation. Gold returns, for example, are overstated since most people buy jewellery and much of the return goes to the jeweller through making charges. Fixed deposit returns turn negative due to taxes and inflation.

Real estate and equity both give positive returns post tax and inflation. But include costs like stamp duty and registration, the cost of fixing the house for a tenant – and the returns from real estate begin to look less attractive. I'm not even including the soul-crushing experience of buying real estate in India – right from the ride that property agents take you on to the black money–lined road to real estate.

## Rules of equity investing

Equity investing has its own rules and unless you follow them, you will lose. One, *when investing in the stock market, give it the same patience you give real estate — a good equity portfolio needs five years of patience, ten years to see consistent returns, but actually will slow-cook over fifteen to twenty years.*

Two, remember that your risk is choosing poor products and finding out after fifteen years that your fund manager has malfunctioned. While others went far ahead, yours did worse than the average product in the market. Three, if you find yourself frozen while choosing equity products in the market — direct stocks, market-linked products such as unit-linked insurance plans (ULIPs) and mutual funds — and don't want to take the risk of choosing a fund manager, go with an exchange-traded fund (ETF) or an index fund linked to a broad market index or a mid-cap index. This is the safest way to get the average market returns without taking the risk of having a fund manager.

You will do worse than the best-managed funds, but better than the worst-managed funds. ETFs also have wafer-thin costs now that the Employees' Provident Fund Organization (EPFO) money into the SBI Mutual Fund ETFs has reduced overall costs for the market.

An average equity fund costs you 2 per cent of the returns a year and the cheapest ETF costs 0.03 per cent. Over a thirty-year period, this difference in cost will be significant if your managed fund does not beat the index by more than the cost difference.

Four, do not invest in any product that locks you into a particular company or asset manager. What we forget is that over the long term in equity investing, the risk is not of the market, but of poor fund management. This is why I do not recommend having a ULIP in your equity portfolio, despite it being competitive with mutual funds in terms of costs.

A ULIP will lock you in with a particular company's asset management and shuffling is expensive. What you want is a product where exit is possible, cheap and easy. Think of it as portability —you should be able to port your money to a better fund manager for a very tiny cost, if you are unhappy with the existing one.

Five, if you want to invest in managed funds, start learning. Go through the Value Research, Morningstar and Crisil ratings. Some smart investors run their funds past all the three metrics to see if they pass the test. Take a considered decision that you can own. Not investing in equity is not an option. You may as well understand the road rules of investing.

Also, remember that we created an emergency fund and bought medical and life covers so that you can put your money to work for the long term. We've taken away the need for keeping money liquid and building a safety net under your money box. Your money box can take the risk that equity brings in the short term now.

So as I make the case for equity, *investors need to remember that if they gave the same respect to equity that they give to real estate, it would be a smoother ride with fewer costs*. Of course, equity investing means that you need to follow the rules.

And rule no. 1 is this: If you want to punt, go to the casino. Getting an equity exposure is about following the rules of holding a portfolio that gives you index-plus returns and not about betting the kitchen sink on a hot tip. If you do that, don't cry later. What's the best way to buy equity? Mutual funds. That's the next chapter.

> You need an equity exposure rather than direct stocks. The best way to expose your money to equity is through mutual funds. Understand that there is a way to get safe equity returns, but you need a plan and you need to manage both greed and fear.
>
> **You are doing okay if**
>
> 1. you understand that equity cooks over time and you need at least seven to ten years of patience to see returns;
> 2. you understand that you will not double your money overnight, but will get a return that is 12–15 per cent a year;
> 3. you understand that mutual funds are the best way to give your money an equity exposure; and
> 4. you understand that if you don't have the ability to choose funds, you invest through index funds or ETFs.

# WHY EQUITY?

Investing in the broad-market index in a growing economy will grow your money over time. Inflation and tax + returns are possible with equity.

**DO NOT INVEST IN EQUITY MARKET FOR YOUR SHORT-TERM GOALS.**

## REAL ESTATE V/S EQUITY

Needs maintenance & timely repairs. Agent fees along with registration, stamp duty and taxes add to costs.

No costs on repair or maintenance. Long-term investors have fewer costs. It is also more liquid than real estate.

## RULES OF EQUITY INVESTING

**1. LET YOUR EQUITY SLOW-ROAST.** Need a time-horizon of at least 7-10 years for returns to show.

**2.** It is time in the market that is important and NOT market timing.

**3.** Individual stock-picking and day-trading are a high-risk way.

**4.** Active mutual funds are good options if you know how to choose well-performing funds.

**5.** Go with an ETF or index fund linked to a broad-market index. It is cheaper and safer.

# 9

# MUTUAL FUNDS

*There is no money box without mutual funds. There is a product for every situation and regulation that puts your interest first.*

A long time ago, a child grew up in a house whose both parents were business journalists, and one of them specialized in personal finance. The kid grew up hearing terms like asset allocation, fiscal deficit, inflation and capital gains. So, in school, they did this exercise, when she was about ten years old.

Imagine that you have Rs 5 lakhs. What will you do with it? Kids did what kids do – they bought dolls, cars, chocolate, Disneyland trips, ice-cream mountains, PlayStations. One kid made a business plan. Rs 3 lakhs for a dog kennel business, Rs 1 lakh in mutual funds, and Rs 1 lakh for two dogs and cats as pets for her.

The dog business will give her Rs 10 lakhs a year. This she would distribute among various family members, and part of it would get her even more pets. Yes, I do think we damaged our kid somewhere – I'm sure this is not normal.

So what are mutual funds? These are also stocks, right? No. They are not. They invest only in equity, right? No. They invest in many things; equity or shares is just one of the many things funds buy. They invest in bonds, gold and also real estate. You can build your entire portfolio by buying mutual funds across these asset classes. And from within the asset class, you can build a diversified portfolio for all your short-, medium- and long-term needs.

Apart from my one house in which I live, some emergency fund FDs, and my PF, all my money is in mutual funds. So, what is a mutual fund and why do I like them so much?

Imagine that you are setting out on a long trip. Think about the way you travel – will you drive your own car, take the train or take a flight? If you drive your own car you need to first know how to drive, know the routes, look after the maintenance of the car and your safety yourself. And, of course, get ready for a long hard drive ahead. If you take a train or a flight, you are handing over the responsibility of getting to your destination to the experts, to the railway and the airline whose job it is to ensure you reach safely on time at a reasonable cost.

Think of investing in a similar manner. You can choose to do it yourself. For that you need to have the time, the knowledge and the capacity to do the work of choosing stocks, building a portfolio and managing it. Or you can hand over the job to professionals whose aim in life is to manage your money.

*A mutual fund is a way to pool the money of a large number of small investors and hand it over to experts to manage it.* Look at it like this: If your monthly saving is Rs 5,000 or Rs 25,000 or even Rs 2 lakhs, trying to find a way to invest it in the market is tough. You have to find the right products, find the time to do the research and then monitor your investments daily.

But if you and thousands of people like you can put your money together, your small contributions can make a very large sum. It can then be handed over to a professional money manager to generate returns. You, as the small investor, could have hired a money manager, but his cost would have been beyond your annual income. When thousands of small investors pool their money, they get the muscle that big money enjoys, in terms of lower cost, because they then buy in bulk, and, of course, the expertise of a fund manager.

But let's understand this creature called a 'mutual fund'. The mutual fund industry in India has a three-part structure. There is a businessman or firm who has the interest to set up a mutual fund. This entity is called a 'sponsor'. There are SEBI rules on who can be a sponsor. The sponsor makes the investment to set up a mutual fund in the hope of making a profit. The sponsor sets up a trust and an asset-management company (AMC). The money collected from investors belongs to a trust. The sponsor appoints the trustees who are the custodians of the investors' money.

The AMC is a service provider to the trust that manages the money for a fee – called AMC fee. The AMC must get all its plans and schemes approved by the trustees before they come to the market. AMCs will launch many schemes to attract investors. Think of it like a car company – it has a variety of car types on offer – from low-end to high-end.

A person who wants to buy a car will match his need for a car to the available car types. A city office goer may settle on a sedan to go to work and back home. A travel freak may choose to buy a four-wheel SUV for those weekend mountain trips. AMCs also launch various schemes and you, the investor, have to choose a scheme that matches your investment objective.

Hmmmm. New words. Investment objective. This is just the reason of your investment. And if you said the only reason was a 'good return', we clearly have work to do.

## All this sounds great, but are they safe?

What is 'safe'? If you mean that your money will not be embezzled, as it was with Hoffland Finance or the emu schemes, or through so many other multilevel marketing scams like Home Trade, yes, your money is safe from the risk of fraud. It is safe from the sponsor running away with it.

A little bit of context. After the Harshad Mehta stock market scam in 1992, there was immense political pressure to put in place watertight rules for retail financial products. The mutual fund industry got liberalized in 1993, with the monopoly of UTI (Unit Trust of India) being broken by the private sector's entry. The rules of the road for private-sector participation ensured that the sponsors or the AMC could not run away with investors' money. Therefore, the money was held by a trust. The rules of trusts in India say that if found guilty, the trustees' personal assets can be attached and they can go to jail. No wonder that no mutual fund has run away with investors' money.

Your money is safe from being stolen. But your money is not safe from the ups and downs of the market – also called volatility. Mutual funds are market-linked products, which means that the current value of the products the fund buys reflects, at the end of the day, in the price, since these products are 'marked to the market'.

We had the big Unit 64 blowout because UTI did not want to follow the SEBI rules on mutual funds and resisted 'marking their portfolio to market'. This means that nobody but insiders in UTI knew the real value of the portfolio. When the portfolio was evaluated at real market prices, it was discovered that there were huge losses that had been hidden.

Many retail investors, especially retired folk, lost their savings in the Unit 64 scam. Till today, people of a certain age resist investing in mutual funds due to the loss of confidence caused by the UTI scam. The government then broke up UTI into two – the good UTI which then followed SEBI's rules and the bad UTI that held all the toxic assets.

The UTI Mutual Fund from which you can now buy schemes is the 'good' UTI. Each time there has been a blowout in the mutual fund industry, the market regulator has come up with tighter and tighter rules to make it safer for retail investors to come to the market.

## So how many kinds of funds are there?

Today you can buy three kinds of asset classes through mutual funds – debt, gold and equity. Real estate is also available through special mutual funds called real estate investment trusts (REITs).

Equity mutual funds buy into stocks of listed companies. Debt mutual funds buy bonds and debt papers issued by the government and firms. Gold funds buy actual gold. Each of these asset classes are further subdivided into categories.

Think of it as a sector called individual vehicles. Within this sector there will be two-wheelers and four-wheelers. Within two-wheelers, there will be motorbikes and scooters. Within motorbikes, there will be high-end and low-end. Within scooters, there will be geared and gearless.

In four-wheelers, there will be small cars, sedans, SUVs (sports utility vehicles), luxury cars. Within each category there will be further subdivisions. You match your budget and need to the vehicle on offer. Think of all the funds out there in a similar manner. There are three broad classifications according to asset type – debt, equity and gold. Within each there are divisions that club similar schemes into groups.

# What are MUTUAL FUNDS?

- Not just stocks -
- Invests in stocks, bonds & gold -

A mutual fund is a way to pool the money of a large no. of small investors and hand it over to experts to manage it.

The sponsor sets up a trust and an asset-management company (AMC).

Collected money is held in the name of the investors by the trust.

The business or firm that sets up a mutual fund is called the sponsor.

AMC manages the money for a fee & launches schemes for investors.

## Is your money safe in a mutual fund?

- Your money is safe from being stolen, but not from market ups & downs.

Each time there has been a blowout in the mutual fund industry, the market regulator (SEBI) has come up with stricter rules to make it safer for retail investors.

How many kinds of mutual funds are there?

### DEBT Funds
Buy bonds & debt papers issued by the government & corporates

### GOLD Funds
Buy actual gold and are called Gold Exchange Traded Funds (ETFs)

### EQUITY Funds
Buy into stocks of listed companies

## Debt funds

Debt funds buy debt papers issued by either the government or firms, or both. What is a debt paper? While there are many kinds of debt papers in the market, we need to understand the basic function of a debt paper – let's call it a bond.

A company needs money for both short-term and long-term needs. It issues bonds. A bond will pay a regular interest to the lender, and then at maturity, it will repay the principal – not very different from the FD that we all know and use.

There are different kinds of bonds according to the time that the money is lent for. There are bonds that mature in a day. There are bonds that mature in thirty years. Long-term bonds are mostly issued by the government. Short-term bonds are issued by both government and companies.

Why not buy bonds directly from the company? We do that in the form of company deposits. And those who have burnt their fingers in this product will swear never to invest in them again. Why's that? Because as an individual, it is very difficult to gauge the health of the business and keep a track of it. It is better to let experts take the call.

Also, think about it in this way. You will buy bonds of one or two or maybe three firms. A mutual fund will hold bonds of at least twenty-five to thirty firms. If one of your three bonds does badly, you lose one-third of your portfolio. If the same bond is held by your mutual fund, the hit on your money will be a fraction, since the fund is holding many other bonds.

*This is called diversification – we reduce our risk by increasing the number of products we hold.* Instead of bonds, our job will then be to choose the right experts from all the mutual funds in the market. And yes, there is a way to do that. But more of that later. We are still learning the alphabet of investing. We'll make words and paragraphs using these lessons later.

So the first thing to remember is that we must buy debt funds to match the investment horizon of the mutual fund scheme with ours. Investment horizon, or the time for which we want to invest our money, can also be called 'tenor'. We are going to match our holding period with that of the scheme we buy.

This means that we will buy a debt fund that invests in short-term bonds if we need our money in the near term. We will buy a debt fund that invests in long-term bonds if we plan to hold the fund for a long time and don't need the money in the near future. We need to understand a bit more about how debt funds are classified before we can invest in them.

## Kinds of debt funds

There are two ways to slice the debt fund market. One, according to tenor, or the holding period of the bond. Two, according to the quality of debt paper bought by the fund.

When you think of a debt fund, ask yourself these two questions. Does the 'average maturity' of the debt fund match my holding period? If I want the money next week, should the average maturity of the fund be three years? Obviously, the answer is no.

Question two is – what quality of debt paper does the scheme hold? The better the quality, the lower will be the potential return. The lower the quality, the higher is the risk and the return. If you don't want risk in your debt fund, settle for debt funds that only buy high-quality paper, and be willing to sacrifice some return for that safety. Unlike what Gordon Gekko said in the movie, I believe that greed is bad – it costs you money.

I will run through two categories of debt funds that I think you should have. There are plenty more, but I don't see the logic of using only a debt product for needs that are more than three to five years away.

## Liquid funds

If there is a banking product that is like a liquid fund, it is the savings deposit. The purpose of a liquid fund is to keep money, well, liquid, or ready for use. The bonds that a liquid fund buys are short-maturity bonds, or bonds that will mature within an average of three months.

'Average maturity' will be a term you will come across when you go to buy a debt fund. All that it means is that the average holding period of all the bonds is about three months in a liquid fund. Other debt funds will have different average maturities. In a liquid fund, some bonds may be maturing tomorrow, some in a week, some in two months and some may mature in four months. The average of all these different maturing dates is three months.

Liquid funds buy short-term bonds. Therefore, the money you have to put in a liquid fund must be money you need in the short term. I keep money in a liquid fund if I know there is an expense coming up in the next three to six months.

SEBI allowed funds in 2016 to make instant redemptions of up to Rs 50,000 a day from liquid funds, or up to 90 per cent of the money in your liquid fund – whichever is lower. If you need the money now, you can go to your fund house website and press sell. The fund will redeem and credit your bank with Rs 50,000 (or less) in no time.

If you have liquid funds with more than one fund house, you can instantly access Rs 50,000 multiplied by the number of liquid funds you hold, no matter whether markets are open or not. Some fund houses have allowed access to liquid funds through a debit card in the past. These are very, very low-risk funds and your capital is quite safe. But you do need to check for something called credit quality of your liquid fund – it must be high to ensure that the money is safe.

A couple of accidents have happened during the 2009 financial crisis, and then the pandemic of 2020, but these are very rare occasions where even banking can freeze. Remember, during demonetization in November 2016, we could not even access our own bank deposits for a long time. Such things happen. It will take a very unusual event to cause you a loss of your invested amount in a good credit quality liquid fund. But is there a guarantee? No.

An even safer option is a fund category called 'overnight funds'. As the name suggests, these schemes buy paper with a maturity of one day. These are the safest but the returns too are very low. These funds are great for treasury managers and entrepreneurs, but for an average household, a good credit quality liquid fund is a better option.

## Money market funds

Money market funds are useful for needs that are within two years from today. These funds invest in bonds that have an average maturity of one year. These carry low levels of risk usually, but you need to constantly watch out for mutual funds buying lower-quality bonds to spike returns. A similar fund category is low duration funds that have an average maturity between six months and a year. You will have to choose your holding period and then match a fund category to it. You can read about these categories in my book *Let's Talk Mutual Funds*.

We read earlier that government bonds are the safest and, therefore, carry the lowest interest rates because there is zero risk of default. In other words, the government will always pay up its debts. But as the risk of non-payment of interest and principal rises, the bonds get graded lower and lower.

If triple-A (AAA) is the safest kind of bond you can buy, a double-B (BB) means fairly high levels of risk. For now, all you need to remember is that if a money market fund is showing very high (compared to the category of money market debt funds) return rates, look deeper into why. It is usually safe to stay with large funds from large well-known fund houses. If you cannot understand this yourself, you definitely need to work with a financial planner, or read more.

## Other types of debt funds

There are other categories of debt funds – low duration funds, corporate bond fund, medium-term bond funds, credit risk funds, long-term bond fund, G-Sec funds and floater funds. For a person beginning the journey of investment, I think you should keep it simple in the beginning, so I won't go into explanations of all the other kinds of debt funds in the market.

Also, I don't think you need any other debt fund product besides the two we talked about at this stage of your journey.

What should you do if your investment horizon is more than two years? You should stay with money market funds, though I might under some circumstances use a conservative hybrid fund due to my higher risk capacity. These are debt funds with a small flavour of equity. The large bond-holding takes away the volatility that equity brings in a bad stock market. But equity adds to the overall returns in a good stock market.

Once you understand mutual funds better, you can switch out of debt funds for cash needs beyond one year or one-and-a-half years and buy hybrid funds too.

Expecting a long-term debt fund to give you returns in the short run is like expecting an airplane to take you to the local market. I remember a conversation I had with a senior officer of the Ministry of Finance. I was a member on the Bose Committee that the government had set up to look at issues of mis-selling and consumer protection in retail finance, and we were discussing investor protection.

The finance ministry mandarin wanted to know why his debt fund was not giving a good return. I asked what he was holding. He had a long-term bond fund and he exited in a year with a loss, because he wanted a long-term product to work in the short term.

Repeat after me: *I need a short-term product for my short-term needs. I need a medium-term product for my medium-term needs. I need a long-term product for my long-term needs.* I must match my investment horizon to that of the fund I buy. My outcome will depend on how well I understand the product I buy. I will not sit in a bullock cart if I need to cover a very long distance. I will not sit in a plane if I need to go across the city. Each of the debt fund categories serves a purpose and can replace the existing products we use.

Why will we replace? We replace them if we get a better return at an acceptable level of risk. You need to remember that debt funds are not risk-free. The risk that you need to watch out for is called 'credit risk'. When your fund buys high-risk papers, it can get a higher rate of interest.

It buys this type of paper to make the fund performance look better. Till the time there is no default, or the borrowing firm pays back interest and principal on time, things are good. But if they default, and the fund has a large amount invested in the firm, you could lose money.

I use debt funds to keep my emergency money, to keep money that I need in the next eighteen months. For horizons more than that, I use a hybrid fund. We'll get to hybrid funds in a bit.

## Gold funds

These are funds that invest in gold. They buy actual gold and track the price of gold in real time. The product is called a gold exchange traded fund (ETF). We'll understand ETFs in just a minute, but for the moment it is enough to know that instead of buying physical gold, you can buy gold that is held by the mutual fund through a gold ETF.

Gold ETFs were launched in 2007 and quickly became popular as investors saw the logic of a good deal. You get lower cost than buying physical gold, you don't have to worry about purity, there are no 'making' charges and it is safer – you don't have to rent a locker to store your gold.

You buy a unit of the gold ETF at the current market price of gold and the ETF invests that money in bullion of 99.55 per cent purity. One unit of an ETF is equal to 1 gram of gold. Gold funds became very popular in India in the great gold rush after the financial crisis of 2008.

What's the cost of this product? You have to pay the cost of a demat account and its brokerage to buy the gold ETF. This usually costs about Rs 1 per lakh for a retail investor with limited trades. The fund house charges an annual cost called expense ratio. This is less than 1 per cent of your assets under management or gold ETFs as in August 2024.

# DEEP DIVE INTO MUTUAL FUNDS

## What are debt funds?

They buy bonds issued by firms, government or both

## Why not buy bonds directly from these companies?

A fund holds many bonds. So you get a diversified portfolio. Reduces risk.

## Kinds of debt funds?

You can look at it in two ways:

1. Tenor or holding period
2. Quality of debt paper bought by the fund

- Higher quality → Lower risk, Lower return
- Lower quality → Higher risk, Potentially higher return

From overnight funds — to — Long-duration funds (10+ years)

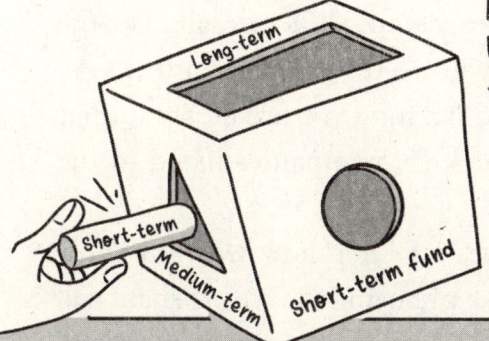

## Match your investment horizon to that of your fund

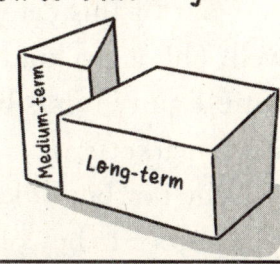

**Gold fund:** Safe way to hold gold investment is through gold ETFs
- no risk of losing physical gold
- but will have costs of demat account & expense ratio

Read the section on understanding expense ratio and how to think about it to get this better.

But falling gold prices and a new product in the market has reduced interest in gold ETFs. The Government of India has launched gold bonds to offer an alternative to gold buyers in the country. Gold imports are a heavy burden on our foreign exchange reserves and sometimes cause a balance-of-payment problem. To allow people to buy gold and yet not cause a loss of foreign exchange, the government has launched the Sovereign Gold Bond Scheme.

Not only is there no cost to the product, investors also get a rate of interest along with a sovereign guarantee. *Remember, the role of gold in your money box is to provide diversification and a hedge against inflation.*

## Equity funds

I love equity funds. They have funded my home renovation and holidays; they have put my kid through college and will see me through my retirement. But to really get the best out of this category you need to understand it very well. This is the kind of mutual fund you are most familiar with. Equity funds buy stocks of companies listed in the stock market.

Why not buy stocks directly? First, how will you know which stock to buy? The risk of buying the wrong share will cost you your peace of mind. When you buy a mutual fund, you outsource the decision to pick stocks to an expert. Fund houses have teams of analysts that track companies, markets, international events, politics and interest rates to see the future of a stock. Based on their reports, the AMC builds your portfolio of stocks.

Why not just buy a blue-chip stock – or maybe three – and sit on it? You can do that but you will have to track the stock to see when it stops being a blue chip. Also, the growth that a blue chip sees may be slower than smaller and more aggressive firms, which also carry higher risk. And sometimes blue chips can tank.

The same diversification that worked for debt funds works here too. The risk of one-third of your money going to zero is very large if all your money is in three stocks. But the equity fund you buy has at least twenty-five to thirty stocks, reducing the impact of a blowout in one stock.

Diversification reduces the negative impact of an imploding stock. And conversely, it reduces the positive impact of an exploding stock. A bit like yoga – you are more balanced, the highs are not that high, the lows not that low. Quite a good place to be in. And not just for money.

## Active and passive funds

Just like debt funds, there are various kinds of equity funds in the market. The first difference to understand is that between 'active' and 'passive' funds. Think of this as the difference between calling a taxi and taking the public transport – metro or a local train – to go to work.

Your experience of the taxi ride will depend a lot on the company you use, the car you choose and the driver you get.

You may reach your destination very fast but the driver may jump red lights, drive too fast and take shortcuts that you are unfamiliar with. You get there faster but you also expose yourself to the risk of a cop catching the driver and causing delay or of an accident. Equally, you won't want a driver who is so cautious on the road that he stops even before the light turns orange. I remember hiring a driver like that once. The guy would not go beyond 30 kmph, and would start slowing down even on green lights.

I'm a very careful driver, and my routine direction to my drivers is that I have plenty of time – no need to rush, so drive safe. But this guy was something else. A journey that takes an otherwise careful driver to complete in thirty minutes took our friend fifty. Needless to say, I got another driver very soon.

Back to mutual funds – you want to be safe, but not be silly safe. When you take the metro, you are taking a very predictable mode of transport. The skill of the driver does not matter that much, and you reach your destination in the time it takes every day. It costs less than a cab but may take longer to reach than the taxi.

An active fund is like the taxi – you are choosing a mutual fund where the fund manager has a view on the market, chooses his stocks to fit the investment mandate, and then manages the money by trading every day. Just as your experience of the taxi ride depends a lot on your driver, so also the performance of an active fund depends a lot on the fund manager. Just as the taxi driver works in the overall corporate environment of a taxi firm – Uber, for instance – so also the fund manager according to the rules set up by the fund.

A taxi driver of a firm that places a very high value on passenger safety will have mechanisms built in to ensure safety. Another firm may value safety less and will have lower standards. Similarly, a fund house may have very good risk-management systems, making the fund manager a safe driver, and another fund house may not. Other than the risk of the market going up and down, or volatility, in an active fund, you also have to deal with the risk of the fund manager taking too many risks or too few.

A passive fund is like taking the metro. You know the cost, you know the distance and you know when you will reach – you don't have to choose the driver, you just need to get to the station and board the right train. A passive fund just buys the index and stays with it. Passive funds don't invest in large research desks, or brokers and dealers, since all they are doing is buying an index and sticking with it. Changes, if any, happen when the composition of the index changes – they sell the outgoing stock and buy the incoming stock. This is why passive funds cost less than active funds.

**Index returns**

Why do we buy active funds when passive is cheaper and less risky? Because the Indian market still has alpha left in it. What's this alpha? Alpha is the extra return that the fund manager can generate over the index. Active fund managers have done very well in India and the higher cost of active management has been more than compensated by the higher returns these have earned.

How does the index give returns, you're thinking. Have you heard the term Sensex return? Or heard somebody say: the Sensex has given returns of 15 per cent a year over the last forty years? What does this even mean? How can the Sensex, which is an index, give returns?

We met Mr Sensex in the last chapter and wanted a way to buy him. The way to do that is through a passive fund. There are two kinds of passive funds – an index fund and an exchange-traded fund. They both choose an index and mimic it.

Let's think of an index fund in the Sensex. We now know that the Sensex has thirty stocks. How many of each is held depends on a formula. So the number of shares of each of the thirty shares that will be bought will depend on the weight of the share in the index.

If we were thinking of a mango price index, we'd include all thirty varieties, and give a higher weight to the kind that sells more. If half the volume of sales came from Alphonso, that kind will have half the weight in the mango index. This is a very crude example, but enough to understand that the Sensex is a weighted average of the prices of thirty stocks.

The index fund will buy the thirty stocks in the same proportion as they have in the Sensex and just stay with the investment. If the Sensex falls by 1 per cent, the index fund's NAV (net asset value, i.e., the price of one unit of a mutual fund) will also fall by around 1 per cent. Your return will be equal to the Sensex return minus costs. Look at the discussion on NAV to understand this better.

An ETF also tracks an index like the Sensex but lists its units on a stock exchange, unlike a mutual fund. To buy and sell mutual funds you don't need to have a demat account. But to invest in an ETF, you need a demat account. The other difference in index funds and ETFs is that you can buy an index fund at a price at the end of the day, but you can buy an ETF at any point in the day. This difference in price is not relevant to retail investors like us.

ETFs come with slightly smaller costs compared to the index funds. The average index fund costs between ten basis points to 1 per cent, or Re 1 to Rs 10 on every Rs 1,000 invested. ETF costs have hit rock bottom and you can now buy them at a price as low as one basis point.

I prefer to stay with index funds for the moment, because the liquidity in the ETFs may not be that good. This means that when you go to sell a large quantity, you may not get the current market price. Remember that things keep changing in the markets and you need to be up to date. If you can't, find a financial planner.

Since there can be any number of indices in a market – broad-market index, mid-cap index, small-cap index, technology index, PSU index, and so on – there can be any number of index funds. Remember that the risk of the index fund you buy will be the risk of the index fund category you buy into. So the risk of a mid-cap index fund is much higher than the risk involved with a Sensex or Nifty fund.

Another way to classify equity mutual funds is by looking at them through the lens of market cap. At the very basic level, there are three kinds of equity funds – large-cap, mid-cap and small-cap funds.

Large-cap funds are more mature and stable, since they invest in the larger companies that are listed in the stock market. A mid-cap fund invests in stocks of mid-sized firms. Small-caps are funds that focus on small companies. Small- and mid-cap stocks are the engines of growth in a portfolio.

These are usually aggressive high-growth firms. The returns from small- and mid-cap firms are much higher than those from large-cap ones, but this possible higher return comes with higher risk. When markets fall, it is the small- and mid-cap stocks that fall harder than the large-cap stocks.

Another classification is called sector funds. These schemes allow you to invest in stocks of a particular sector – technology, banking, pharma, FMCG and retail. Then there are thematic funds that track a bunch of sectors. For instance, the infrastructure theme will include sectors such as construction, telecom, power and so on. So a sector fund is a narrower cut of the market; a thematic fund a broader cut.

You ask me which has more risk. Right, the sector funds are riskier. Each of these categories can have an active fund or a passive fund. What is a diversified equity fund? This is one term you would have heard if you ever read personal finance pages of a newspaper or switched on a business channel. Exactly as the term says – this is a fund that is diversified across mainly large-cap stocks. These funds aim to give returns that are just a bit higher than the index.

Another classification you will hear is open-ended and closed-end funds. Think of an open-ended fund like a very long unending escalator and a closed-end fund like a lift. You can get on and off the escalator any time you want, but once you get in the lift you can only get off on the floor whose button you pressed.

An open-ended fund is forever open for investors buying and selling it. A closed-end fund comes to the market with a fixed time frame. Closed-end equity funds come with a fixed-year investing horizon. I like open-ended funds that have been in the market for at least five years. I like to see the report card of the past to see if I can trust the fund manager and the fund house with my money.

I know this is a lot of work, but once you get familiar with the terms, it will become easier. You are preparing for a lifetime of investment and not just a one-time hit and run number. When I joined Iyengar Yoga a couple of years ago to fix a really bad lower back and a general loss of mobility, the first few months were spent in terror. I simply could not remember the names and postures of all the asanas the yoga teacher was throwing at us.

But I was in this for the long haul. I knew that yoga is my road to recovery, so I persisted, and slowly, as I engaged more and more with it, it got easier. The names of the asanas now roll off my tongue just as easily as finance jargon! So stay with this. It will do your financial health a whole lot of good to just understand the terms the *Suits* throw at you.

## Growth or dividend*

There are three kinds of options that each mutual fund scheme offers you: growth, dividend and dividend reinvestment. The growth option allows you to stay invested and get the benefit of long-term growth of the portfolio. Your profits are not 'realized', or in other words, your profits reflect in the rising price, much like a stock price that goes up. Till you sell, the profit is 'unrealized' or notional. The growth option works especially well for equity funds as it allows you to keep the money invested in the market. The profit your fund makes remains in the market and you get the benefit of compounding over the years. The number of units you buy remain the same, but the price, or the NAV, keeps going up.

I remember twenty years ago when mutual funds were still new, and I was hesitating to invest. I now wish I had just put Rs 1 lakh in one of the early schemes in the market. Invested in 1993, that money is worth more than Rs 1 crore,

---

* SEBI, in 2021, changed the name of dividend plan to income distribution with capital withdrawal to better reflect the option. Read my book *Let's Talk Mutual Funds* to understand this better.

an annual average growth of 19 per cent. This option is good for those who don't need an income from their investment today but are targeting a corpus for future use.

The dividend option is not really the dividend, but booked profits. This option allows you to book profits periodically. The number of units remain the same, but the NAV keeps reflecting the booked profits. Obviously for the same scheme, the NAV of a growth option will be higher than the dividend option. This option is good for those who need a periodic income from their investments, like the retired do. The dividend reinvestment option is a strange animal that wants growth but is afraid of not booking profits.

A legacy of the past, the dividend reinvestment option is unique to India. What happens is this: Profits are booked, but instead of declaring a dividend, the fund house buys more units at the current price. So your number of units goes up but the NAV remains near the dividend option NAV. In effect you have the growth option corpus. It used to be an option to manage taxes, but subsequent tax changes have taken that advantage away. Stay with growth funds for most of your needs and use a systematic withdrawal plan (SWP) to draw money as you need it. This is a good option for some tax manoeuvring in debt funds. Do talk to your tax consultant on how to use it.

## What is an ELSS?

If you pay income tax, you will be familiar with this product called the equity-linked savings scheme. You know that if you contribute to certain products, like the premium of a life insurance policy, or the public provident fund (PPF), or units of an ELSS scheme, you get a deduction from your taxable income. In August 2024, the benefit was Rs 1.5 lakhs.

An ELSS is an equity fund that gets this tax benefit. It has a three-year lock-in period, and you cannot exit before that. Remember *not* to tick the dividend or dividend reinvestment option in an ELSS. Go for growth. Work out why that is a good idea.

## Balanced funds*

As the name suggests, a balanced fund is a hybrid. It's like a mango duet ice cream. The joy of mango along with vanilla ice cream on a stick! It remains one of my all-time favourite ice-cream bars. Right after the orange bar. Orange bars are the most … OK, sorry, back to funds.

Today there are three kinds of balanced funds – conservative, balanced and aggressive. Conservative funds have between 10 and 25 per cent in equity, balanced have between 40 and 60 per cent in equity and aggressive 65–80 per cent in equity. Conservative balanced funds used to be called monthly income plans (MIPs) but SEBI disallowed this saying that it was misleading.

---

* On 1 April 2021, SEBI changed the name of balanced funds to hybrid funds to better reflect the category. Read about this in detail in my book *Let's Talk Mutual Funds*.

Remember that these are not assured income schemes; they are just debt funds with a small crust of equity to give a slightly higher return than a pure debt fund. Balanced funds are a great first investment to make in order to taste equity funds. There are many other kinds of funds in the market. For a beginner, the discussion here is enough.

## NAV

What is this NAV? It is the price of a unit of a scheme. The full form is net asset value. It is not 'gross', because the costs have been removed from the price, and you get the net value in your hand. Imagine there are 100 investors and each has put in Rs 1,000 in an equity mutual fund.

Each bought a unit for the price of Rs 10; therefore, each investor holds 100 units. A sum of Rs 1 lakh is invested by the mutual fund in different stocks. A year later, the value of the portfolio is Rs 1.5 lakhs, giving a profit of Rs 50,000. This will be shared equally by the units, but before that, costs will be removed. If the cost is Rs 10,000, the profit that goes to the unit holders is Rs 40,000. This gets reflected in the NAV that goes from Rs 10 to Rs 14. Your 100 units are now worth Rs 1,400. Multiply the NAV with the number of units you hold to get the value of your mutual fund holding per scheme.

## How do mutual funds make money?

Good question. Nobody is doing charity here. Profit motive with good regulation is the best way for competition to flower and for the consumer to get a good deal. Costs matter and you need to understand costs really well so you can decode not just mutual funds but other products as well.

Remember that costs don't really matter in a fixed-return product, such as a fixed deposit (FD) or a bond. A 10 per cent FD will give 10 per cent on the principal. The banks price the deposit after taking care of their costs and profits.

Bonds and traditional plans (non-participating plans only) sold by insurance companies too work on the same logic – you get a defined amount back either periodically or in one bullet shot some ten to fifteen years later. You need to just worry about the rate of interest, the final payback and the current inflation rates.

But you need to think about costs in a market-linked product or one in which the returns are linked to an underlying asset such as stocks, bonds, real estate, gold or commodities.

In its simplest form, a market-linked investment product carries three kinds of costs. One, the cost to enter the product, also called a front load. If you invest Rs 100, and Rs 2 from that is cut out so that Rs 98 is invested, the Rs 2 is called a load.

A load is part of the price of the product, or is embedded in the price – it is an invisible charge because it is not usually disclosed. Mutual funds have zero loads and are an extremely investor-friendly product. The question to ask when buying a market-linked investment product is: How much of the money I invest goes to work?

Two, an ongoing cost or the annual fees that you need to pay to have experts manage your money. To take care of the running costs and profits of investment managers each year, some fees are deducted from your money. The cost to you of handing over your money to professionals is captured in a number called the 'expense ratio'. This is the fees that a mutual fund charges investors for its costs and the profits it makes.

The market regulator has put ceilings on how much a fund can charge you. This charge varies across fund categories. For example, a liquid fund may charge as little as 13 paise to 70 paise for every Rs 100 invested every year. Debt funds such as ultra-short-term funds charge more, and it typically varies from 50 paise to Rs 1.60 on every Rs 100 in the scheme. Equity funds can cost more depending on the category of the funds. For example, large-cap non-index funds can cost from Rs 1.47 to almost Rs 2.62 as in August 2024. Small-cap funds, for example, cost between Rs 1.43 and Rs 2.50, per Rs 100 invested. These are costs for managed (non-index) regular plans. Index funds, ETFs and direct plans cost much less. We'll discuss direct plans in a minute.

These numbers may look small but they add up to be a significant amount over the years – both for you and for the fund. For example, the difference between an expense ratio of 0.5 per cent and 1.5 per cent over a twenty-year period is huge.

If you bought an equity fund and got a twenty-year annual pre-cost return of 15 per cent a year, the fund with the lower expense ratio will get you a net return of 14.5 per cent, and the higher expense ratio will give you 13.5 per cent. What difference does that make? If you had Rs 1 lakh invested in both, one scheme will give you Rs 15 lakhs, and the other will give you Rs 12.58 lakhs. Costs matter. Do look at the expense ratios of the funds you buy.

Three, an exit cost, or the cost of selling the product. To take care of expenses of selling the investment you made or to act as a deterrent to frequent churning of money, funds levy exit charges. This is a percentage of your corpus and usually falls off to zero after about one or two years. Ask this question: What does it cost to redeem this product after one, two, three years, and so on, over the life of the product?

## What is a direct plan?

The expense ratio has embedded in it the sales commission paid to sellers of mutual funds. There are two entities in the market – advisers and distributors. Distributors are supposed to just vend the product, much as a chemist vends medicines but does not prescribe them. For prescription, you go to a doctor, who charges a fee.

In the financial sector, advisers are the doctor's equivalent and are supposed to charge you a fee for their expertise. They are supposed to recommend a 'direct' plan that has a lower cost. Direct plans remove the sales commission embedded in the expense ratio and make the product cheaper for you to buy. For example, a large-cap direct fund will cost 0.55 per cent and the same fund as a regular fund will cost 1.54 per cent. If you've understood NAVs and expense ratio, you will know why the NAV of a direct plan will become higher than that of a regular plan. If not, read this part one more time. Do some numbers to get the concept right.

## SIPs and more

Why is everybody I meet talking about SIPs? What's this cool new thing, and should I be SIP-ing? A SIP is a systematic investment plan. Think of this as a recurring deposit, but instead of putting money in a fixed deposit, you are making periodic investments into a mutual fund.

Using the vehicle of an SIP is good for two big reasons. One, we usually earn a fixed amount each month and have a monthly surplus left over after expenses. An SIP is a good way to soak up the savings each month. Some people make a target for saving in an SIP and then spend the rest. They make SIP investments a target rather than a residue.

An SIP matches the earning rhythm of most people and is very useful in building the habit of regular investment. Two, an SIP allows you to average out your price as you invest over the year, either monthly, or fortnightly, or even quarterly. Since nobody can predict the market, making one large lump-sum investment leaves us open to the risk of a sudden market crash. Spacing out investments over the year allows our money to buy more when markets are down and less when markets are hot.

Do you know that people like us are pumping over Rs 21,000 crores a month (that's more than a trillion rupees a year!) into the equity market through SIPs as in June 2024? And do you know that people like us are the reason Indian markets don't fall when foreign hot money flows out? *But remember that SIP is a vehicle and not the goal. You use an SIP to make investments in a mutual fund.* You can choose any scheme and build an SIP ladder into it. That fund, you still have to choose either yourself or by hiring a financial adviser.

A systematic transfer plan (STP) is a facility that allows you to space out a big investment over time. Remember we read that investing every month is better than hitting the market with a large lump sum? What if you suddenly got a big bonus or some arrears, or inherited a bunch of money? Instead of investing it all in one go, you can put the money in a liquid fund and set up a monthly (or weekly or fortnightly) transfer into an equity scheme. Remember that you have to choose a liquid fund of the same fund house whose equity fund you want to buy through an STP.

A systematic withdrawal plan (SWP) is a facility to periodically redeem your units to generate an income. Yes, it works like a dividend plan, but in this case the control remains in your hand of how much money you want to take from your fund periodically. The risk in an SWP is of it eating into your corpus. I find an SWP a useful tool for my retired father who is in a mix of debt and equity funds.

I can actually go on about mutual funds. But let's stop here. You have the basic building blocks of making a portfolio using mutual funds and that is enough for now. We are now getting to the point of actually making decisions for the money box on what to put in it. We're reaching here after doing all the hard work and not falling for a smart sales pitch of your bank manager. Let's fill that money box with all good things!

> The best way for average households to invest for short-, medium- and long-term goals, mutual funds have an array of product types. Not just equity, funds invest also in debt and gold.
> 
> **You are doing okay if**
> 
> 1. you understand that you can invest in debt, equity and gold through mutual funds;
> 2. you understand that managed funds cost more, carry more risk, but also can give higher returns;
> 3. you understand that the lowest cost and safest way to get an equity exposure is to use index funds or ETFs that track the Sensex or Nifty50; and
> 4. you understand that churning your mutual fund portfolio benefits the seller and not you and, therefore, you should choose carefully and stay invested for years.

# EQUITY FUNDS

Broadly, mutual funds are of the following types:

**1. Active funds**

Fund manager chooses stocks and bonds

**2. Passive funds**

Fund mimics an index

↓

2a. Exchange traded funds listed on the stock market

2b. Index funds

---

## What to choose—growth or dividend?

### Growth
- Allows you to stay invested
- Profits are not realized until you sell
- Number of units remain same
- NAV grows

### Dividend
- Allows you to book periodic profit
- For people needing periodic income e.g., retired folk
- Number of units reduces
- NAV falls after distribution

### Dividend reinvestment
- Booked profits buy more units at current price
- Number of units increases
- NAV remains near dividend option

Note: Dividend options now called income distribution with capital withdrawal

---

## Should you be <u>SIP</u>-ing?

Systematic investment plan

A periodic investment into a mutual fund

1. Allows you to build a habit of regular investing

2. Allows you to average out the price as you invest monthly/fortnightly or quarterly

# 10

# PUTTING IT ALL TOGETHER

*Each product you buy must fight for its place in your money box.*

The food is now cooked. The rice, chapatti, dal, vegetables, fish, chicken, dahi, pickle, papad and sweets are all sitting in their containers. Who eats what and how much is a function of individual tastes and needs. A fifteen-year-old can eat however much of whatever. More likely she'll order pizza, sniffing in disdain at today's unexciting lunch. Let teenagers be, and let's talk about a thali meal. Each food type has a certain place on the thali.

For example, you can't just make a meal of the pickle or the papad. You need the base of carbohydrates in the roti and rice. You need the protein in the dal and the meat. You need the minerals and vitamins in the veggies. You need the probiotics in the dahi. The pickle and the papad are the taste-kickers to give an extra heft to your meal.

Look at the different financial products as different food types – each has a role and solves a specific problem. You don't just buy a product because it is sold to you. *Each product in your money box needs to justify its space. It has to fight with other products available to claim its place in your money box.* The time has come to now begin filling the money box with products.

There are some basic features of a financial product that you must understand. We think finance is tough but it is actually not. We don't need the rocket science deals. We just need products we can understand.

How do you understand something that is not visible? A financial product is invisible and is created when the person selling it describes it, or when it is described in a brochure or website. We need to evaluate a financial product's features. What are the most important features? The sellers will talk up all kinds of features, but at the very basic level, an investment-oriented financial product must be evaluated on six parameters.

## Cost

What does it cost me to buy this product? When we buy an insurance policy or a mutual fund, it is not very obvious that there is a cost. Financial products have at least three kinds of costs that you must know about. First, there is a cost to buy the product. Look at this as an entry ticket, a ticket that allows you to board the bus. Different products, even if they do the same thing, have different entry costs, also called loads. These are commissions that the person selling collects from the manufacturer of the financial product.

Understand that in certain kinds of life insurance products, like endowment and money-back plans, the cost of buying the product can be as high as 75 to 100 per cent as in August 2024. If your premium is Rs 1 lakh, your entire premium can go as commission to the agent selling it to you. In addition, they charge 'policy administration charges' or the cost to the insurance company to make that sale. Does this explain the hard sell you face on life insurance products?

In a ULIP the front load is about 8–9 per cent. In a mutual fund, there is no cost of entry. The front load was brought to zero in 2009. In a bank FD, PPF and PF, there is no front load. The National Pension Scheme (NPS) has very small costs of entry. Front costs reduce the money that goes to work in a financial product. These also encourage the sellers to 'churn' you, or nudge you to sell your old product and keep buying new ones.*

Second, there is an ongoing cost. This is the money you need to pay each year for you to stay in the product. Also

---

* You have been 'churned' when an insurance agent makes you stop funding an old policy and sells you a new one. He has already harvested the high first-year commission on the old policy, the subsequent commissions drop to 7.5 per cent, and will now harvest the commission on the new one. Commissions go down over time on life insurance products and, therefore, the incentive to keep selling you newer policies. Stockbrokers also churn direct stock investors because they make money each time they buy and sell. Therefore, brokers encourage people to trade on the stock market rather than invest.

called expense ratio, this is usually a percentage of the money in the investment. If you invested Rs 1 lakh and the money is now worth Rs 2 lakhs, you will pay the expense ratio on Rs 2 lakhs. The expense ratios differ according to the type of product you buy. They are low for debt-oriented products and high for equity-oriented products.

Ask the seller: What does this product cost annually to hold? Remember that the fund manager makes money even when you make a loss. That's the nature of financial products.

Third, the cost of exiting the product, or an 'exit load', which is the cost the fund manager charges to take care of the costs of exit. Most debt funds have zero exit cost, and most equity funds have an exit cost of 1 per cent if you leave before one year. Exit costs are very high for insurance products – if you leave midway, you lose a big chunk of your money. Till 1 October 2024, if you exited the policy after one premium, you got nothing back. Even after five years, you got just half your capital back. New regulations have increased surrender values making the product less toxic.

We must learn to look at costs of a financial product differently than the cost of a car or a packet of chips. When you buy a packet of chips (visible) or even a mobile plan (invisible), the seller has a sales commission embedded in the price that he charges you. We don't worry too much about these commissions because if you don't like the chips or the mobile service, you simply go to another brand next time.

*But a financial product is usually a long-term deal and you will find out maybe five to ten – or even thirty – years later (pension products, for example) if the product was good for you or not.* Commissions in investment products encourage sellers to maximize their income rather than your financial well-being. Therefore you need to choose products with zero or very tiny front costs. Ongoing costs over a long period also will cost you a lot.

For example, the difference of just 1 percentage point in costs can reduce your final corpus by almost 30 per cent over a thirty-year period. We don't worry about costs in a guaranteed-return product like the FD, because you buy the product on the basis of the net return that is disclosed.

## Return

What does it return? The purpose of an investment product is to give you a return. You should know what a product returns, either definitely in a guaranteed product, or approximately in a market-linked one. Stay away from products that give you returns in absolute numbers – Rs 1 lakh will become Rs 5 lakhs. This does look like a return of five times, but when you understand that this is over thirty years, the return works out to an unimpressive 5.5 per cent a year.

Also remember that returns and risk are linked. Low returns usually come with a guarantee. To get a higher return, you will need to take more risk. Stay away from low-return market-linked products like participating insurance plans. Remember the return must be in terms of your investment. A trick to fool you perfected by insurance companies is to link returns to a third number!

The agent will tell you: You will get back 105 per cent of the sum assured – 105 per cent looks like a big number. But the sum assured is not your investment, it is the death benefit! Beware of such illustrations and sales pitches. You should be able to compare the return to your bank FD. Market-linked products and 'participating' insurance plans cannot give assurances of future returns, so ask to see how the product did on past returns. Don't let the seller shop for the best-return year.

In a mystery shopping exercise I did for a research paper in 2015 with economist Renuka Sane, we sent mystery shoppers to 400 bank branches in Delhi, and found bank managers picking the best past return to lure investors.

Ask for an average annual return of the product for the last three, five and ten years. Then ask to see benchmark returns. Then ask to see category returns.

Category return is the average return of the category of the product. For example, if the seller tells you that your money will go into a large-cap fund, even in a ULIP, ask to see what the category of large-cap funds have done over the past. How does the fund being sold compare to that?

What about participating plans that lure with a 'bonus'? As I said earlier, the use of the word bonus is simply a trick and a trap. To lure and trap you in a low-return product. Ask what similar plans have returned in the past as a percentage of the total amount invested. If the seller can't answer, walk away from the product.

## Lock-in

Is there a lock-in? This is important to know. A lock-in means that you cannot withdraw your money for a certain period of time. For example, the lock-in with the PPF product is fifteen years. The lock-in with a five-year bank FD is, well, five years.

Mutual funds are of two types, open-ended and closed-end. There is no lock-in in open-ended funds, but closed-end equity funds have a lock-in, usually three to five years. The ELSS funds are locked in for three years. Open-ended funds may not have a lock-in, but can have a cost of exiting before a certain period of time (more of that in the next section). ULIPs have a five-year lock in.

Traditional plans don't have a lock-in, which means you can stop funding the policy whenever you want, but the policy tenure could be ten, fifteen or even thirty years. Don't confuse the premium-paying term with the policy tenure.

Sellers of insurance lie about this feature and make you think that a five-year premium-paying term is the policy tenure. Tenure is usually much, much longer. NPS has an age-linked lock-in – you cannot redeem before you hit age sixty. I like to invest for the long-term, but don't like lock-ins. They force me to stay with a poorly performing fund manager. What happens if I exit early?

## Cost to exit early

Early exit can happen in two ways. One, you want to exit before the lock-in gets over. For example, in PPF, what if you want to stop the product midway and get your money back? Or you want to redeem your money before three years in an ELSS fund? Or you want to redeem your money from a ULIP before five years? Or exit the NPS or your PF?

Well, you can't. There are some special circumstances in which you can redeem a part of the NPS or your PF. A closed-end mutual fund does have an exit option before the tenure because it is listed on a stock exchange and you can get the current NAV if you sell your fund on the exchange. But historically, listed closed-end funds trade below their NAV, and most investors prefer to wait it out. Anyway, if you have a good emergency fund, your need for midway liquidity should be adequately met.

Two, what happens when you exit a long-term product? You need to ask: Is there a cost to an early exit? For example, if you want to exit from a three-year bank deposit in two years, you can do that, but it usually costs you 0.5 per cent of interest. Products like equity mutual funds, ULIPs and endowment plans should be bought with an investment horizon of at least five to thirty years. What happens if you exit earlier than the product term?

In open-ended mutual funds exit costs are used to keep investors in the product for a minimum amount of time. This is done using an 'exit load'. For example, liquid funds are like the savings deposit and there is no exit load. Most ultra-short-term funds don't have an exit load. Credit risk funds and debt funds that buy lower-quality paper to give a return kicker, usually have a 1 to 4 per cent (that is, it will cost you 1 to 4 per cent of your money in the product as a cost to exit before a year. If you had Rs 5 lakhs in a fund with an exit load of 1 per cent, and you exit before one year, then you'd pay Rs 5,000 on exit. You would get back Rs 4,95,000 if you exited before one year) before a holding period of 365 days as an exit load.

Equity funds usually cost 1 per cent if you exit before a year, but this can vary. Do ask: What is the exit load and the period that would be considered an early exit? Or look it up on the Value Research website.

In a ULIP, if you want to redeem before five years, it costs you a maximum of Rs 6,000 – your money will move to a 'discontinuation fund' and still earn you a minimum interest. If you stop paying premiums after five years and want to redeem your investment, you will get the current NAV of your fund.

The biggest cost to your money has been through traditional plans till 1 October 2024. Till then, if you did not pay the second premium, after paying the first, you got nothing back. Early exits now cost much less, but are still a very high-penalty when compared to mutual funds or bank deposits.

India's learned insurance regulator has allowed insurance companies to appropriate your money as 'costs' for decades before changing the rules. These used to be booked as profits after two years some time ago. If you have heard of the term 'lapsation profit', you know that some of the profits of life insurance companies came from the money you lost when you lapsed on your policy. Find out what it costs to exit earlier than the product term. In the mystery shopping story mentioned earlier, when our auditors asked about the costs of exit, over two-thirds of the bank managers did not answer the question. Either they did not know or were not willing to tell. Ask your seller to write down what it costs to exit and over what time period.

## Holding period

Do you look at boiling milk and making kheer with the same time period in mind? Milk is a five-minute job and kheer cooks slowly to become the wonderful sweet it is. Each financial product has a use-by date on it. Unfortunately, regulators in India do not force manufacturers or sellers to put that date on the product material.

If you use a financial product that releases its flavour over many years for a short-term need, you are courting financial disaster. Therefore, planners do not recommend pure equity products for financial goals that are less than three years away. *Each product you allow into your money box must answer this question: How long do I need to hold it for it to work for me?*

This is one of the most crucial questions to ask, because the success or failure of a financial product is also dependent on whether you bought a product that is suited for your investment horizon.

There are some products that even if held to term are bad for your money box. I will include ULIPs and traditional plans in this category. *Do not bundle investment and insurance.* Keep your investment cells of the money box free of the scourge of a bundled life insurance plan.

## Taxes

Returns need to be evaluated taking into account the costs, inflation and taxes. Once these three big bites are taken out of your returns, most products give a negative return. Taxes can be levied at various points in a product. And some products give you a tax break if you invest in them.

The most well-known tax break is Section 80C, which gives you a break of up to Rs 1.5 lakhs (in 2024) if you invest in the eligible products. You get this break if you contribute to your PF, PPF, life insurance premiums, ELSS mutual funds, NPS, special five-year FDs and a bunch of other expenses.

The ideal time to begin your Rs 1.5 lakh investment is from the beginning of the financial year, and not in February or March just before the year closes. It is a good idea to use your Rs 1.5 lakh investment in your PF (NPS, if you don't have PF), PPF, your term insurance premium and ELSS funds. Other than the NPS tax benefit, none of these deductions are available in the new tax regime that has lower rates of taxation but no provision for deduction benefits.

You also need to know if the return is taxed. Is there a tax to be paid on the interest, dividend or profit of that particular product? And, finally, is there a tax on exit. The interest on your bank FD, for example, will get added to your income and be taxed at your slab rate.

The rules around how dividends are taxed keep changing, so do look up the latest tax impact. As of August 2024, they are taxed at slab level in the hands of the investor.

Then there are two kinds of 'capital gains' that you need to be aware of. Short-term and long-term capital gains. In a debt fund, earlier than 2023, if you sold before three years of holding the fund, you had to pay a short-term capital gain tax on the profit. This profit got added to your income and you paid tax at slab rate on it. If you held for three or more years, your profit would become long-term and you paid a tax that was usually lower than the highest tax rate on income. These rules changed in 2023 and as in August 2024, debt funds are taxed at slab level.

Equity used to enjoy a special place in the taxman's heart and holding equity for one year made it a 'long-term' product and it became tax-free. However, that has changed from 1 April 2018 and long-term capital gains from equity began to be taxed at 10 per cent, after a threshold of Rs 1 lakh in profit. Budget 2024 has hiked this to 12.5 per cent with Rs 1.25 lakh as tax-free profit.

If you redeem an equity fund within a year of buying (which you should not, but if you do), and you make a profit, you pay a short-term capital gains tax on the profit. This rate is at 20 per cent as in August 2024, after Budget 2024 hiked it from 15 per cent. Again the rates and surcharges keep changing, so look up the latest tax rates.

Life insurance policies with investment embedded in them enjoy tax-free status on exit. Returns from equity ULIPs are now taxed above a certain threshold of premium. Again, these rules change often so check with the tax site for the latest. Remember that most plans from insurance compare unfavourably with PPF, bank deposits and mutual funds.

## Asset allocation

We've now asked all the questions and have a short list of products we want to use. Can we finally begin to fill our money box with investment products? Yes, but only after we understand what asset allocation means. Think of asset allocation as a way of reducing your risk. Diversification of a portfolio is achieved through asset allocation. Too much jargon already.

Think about what you eat in a day. Do you eat only one thing or do you try and balance it out? A mix of roti, rice, meat, veggies, fruit, milk, dahi, junk, juice, fizzy, alcohol and whatever more is what an average person will ingest in a day. We eat too much, but I am digressing again. Back to finances.

What'll happen if you only eat pizza morning, noon and night? Apart from getting bored in a week, your body will begin to protest the lack of diversity in the diet. Think of your finances in a similar way. Just one kind of product is harmful to the portfolio because it concentrates your risk in just one thing. Did you say FDs were fine for my dad and they'll be fine for me – where's the risk in an FD?

Sure, no risk of markets crashing, you will get your interest and principal back; but what about the loss due to inflation? You know that when governments borrow too much money, they use the tool of inflation to reduce the real value of their debt.

They reduce the purchasing power of your money as they inflate away their debt. After the 2008 farm-loan waiver in India, inflation went to double digits as the government used inflation to reduce its liabilities. Inflation is a serious risk for you if all your assets are sitting in FDs.

Look at your dad today – is he managing fine without help from the kids? Unless he is on a government pension, chances are that he is not. What worked for your dad need not work for you.

You need a mix of assets in your portfolio. Debt gives you the stable core. Include products like your PF, PPF, FDs, bonds and debt funds in the debt part of your portfolio. Equity gives the return kicker – it is the only asset class that gives you returns that beat inflation, at the lowest cost. You can include gold in this, for diversification.

Keep about 5–10 per cent at the most of your net worth in gold if you want to. The exact asset allocation between debt and equity will vary from person to person. *The thumb rule for equity is 100 minus your age.* If you are thirty years old, you should have 70 per cent of your money in equity. If you are sixty years old, you should have 40 per cent of your money in equity. Yes, you need equity even when you retire.

Each of your goals will need their own allocation between debt and equity. For example, the goal of retirement that is thirty years away may have an allocation of 100 per cent equity, but a goal for a kids' education that is five years away could have an allocation of 70 per cent debt and 30 per cent equity. Again, asset allocation depends on your risk appetite and capacity. The thumb rule is this: the closer you are to the goal, the lesser should be the equity part of your portfolio. Remember that we are over-invested in real estate and debt and have very little equity allocation.

## A product for every cell

It is time to put a product in every cell. I won't give you product names but will give product types. Financial products are dynamic and will need an update once in a while. It's best you either do your own research or work with a financial planner to get the exact product names.

But how do you know how to save for which goal? Although there are plenty of calculators online that will help with doing the numbers, for this third edition, I have included worksheets at the end of the book that help you calculate your own numbers. Use the learnings from here to plug and play with your own unique financial numbers and needs.

## Cash-flow cell

You need three bank accounts when you are starting out. As you get more used to the cash-flow system, you can use just two. Your salary account is your Income Account where all inflows drop.

The Spend-It Account can be a joint account with your partner or parent or child – whoever shares the routine household expenses with you.

It is a good idea for both partners to contribute to running of the house. It is usual for a woman to use her salary to run the house and the man his to build the assets. Unfortunately, in a divorce situation, the law awards assets to the person that paid for them. So share the routine expenses and build assets in both names.

The third account is the Invest-It Account into which you move either the leftover money from expenses as savings or the amount you target each month towards investments. Remember to choose banks that have excellent interfaces – both mobile and online – and good security systems.

The bank accounts should be such that they should allow you to link up with the various money transfer applications now available. Going online and linking your Invest-It Account to various financial product-vending platforms is key to the smooth running of your money box.

It took me full six months to set it up. The passwords were missing, some banks needed additional security measures before I could transact and so on. So it is good to test it out for a few months to iron out all the glitches. Today, it takes me less than thirty seconds to make an investment or redeem it. Remember we are trying to get your time free for things that matter.

Those used to mutual funds may want to keep a part of their monthly spending money in a liquid fund. There are funds that allow an instant redemption of up to Rs 50,000 from a liquid fund into your savings deposit or allow access through a debit card. Especially, if your expenses are large and you find your savings deposit quite full till about the fifteenth of the month – put part of the spending money in a liquid fund.

## Emergency cell

When we need the money from this cell, we'll need it in a hurry – usually within a week or ten days. Even if you face a job loss, you usually get at least three months' severance pay. Therefore, we need products that earn a little more than a simple savings deposit, but is easy to break.

You have a choice between two products. The first is the reliable FD. We know these products; we find them safe and know how to get in and out of them. Just the familiarity and the ease of on- and off-boarding makes an FD a contender for the emergency fund cell. You can pick the period for the FD that gives the highest interest from a large scheduled commercial bank – private or public.

At times, the three-year FD gives more than the five-year FD. There is a cost of about 0.5 per cent of interest for an early exit from an FD. It is worth it to pay that and keep the money in an FD rather than a savings deposit that gives you an interest between 2.7 and 4.25 per cent, as in August 2024. You can use a flexi account that some banks offer to have the facility to sweep out the money you need from the FD into the savings deposit instantly. But that also increases the chances of you dipping into the emergency funds for an impulse purchase.

The second product is a mutual fund. I keep my emergency money in a mix of FDs and debt funds. Choose a fund that is conservative and not aggressive. This means that you shouldn't buy a product for your emergency cell based on just the high returns it has given in the past.

To harvest more returns, fund managers of some fund houses take 'credit risk' or invest in poorer grade bonds than the others. If you are buying yourself, check that the top holdings of your debt fund is in AAA-rated bonds. If you are investing through an agent or adviser, ask her to ensure that your safety is not compromised for returns.

Once you understand mutual funds and get used to investing in them, you may even move your emergency money to a conservative hybrid fund. But that is a decision you take after talking to your partner. I would love to make the transition to a higher-risk product for my emergency fund, but my husband is seriously risk-averse. So to keep domestic harmony, we sit in safer funds for this cell.

Finance is not just about numbers; it should work for all the people in the house and must look after individual preferences, fears and goals. If a product leaves one person feeling insecure, the product is not worth it. You can either convince the partner or stay with the lower-risk product.

## Medical insurance cell

This is a really tough one. You need either a really good financial planner who will choose for you, or you need some kind of help to compare policies so that you can choose the right one. Take the help of league tables put out by third-party entities such as newspapers. Be careful with online portals that may have ratings that are compromised.

Medical cover is needed as the costs of hospitalization have gone through the roof. Unfortunately, in India, hospitals are unregulated and are charging whatever they want. This results not just in higher costs when you pay the bill but also in higher insurance premiums. Depending on your need, this cell gets a medical insurance policy that insures you and your family against hospital bills.

## Life insurance cell

I don't want to see a single ULIP, money-back, endowment, whole life policy in this cell. We went over the reasons in the chapter on life insurance why a term plan is the only way to build security for the family against your untimely death.

Life insurance bundled with investments are very high-cost products that benefit the agents, banks and life insurance firms more than they benefit you. Shut your ears to the hard sell, or cut the loss and stop funding these policies. Ask any good financial planner in India and the one big mistake they find in their clients' portfolios when they take them on is too many of these useless products.

You need a term plan to cover just the risk of you having an untimely death. You need between eight to ten times your annual income as a cover. You need to also cover any loan that you have. Car, credit card, personal, education, home – add these up and buy an additional term plan to cover the loans. You don't want your spouse to be paying EMIs on the home loan you did not protect.

Look for a combination of a low premium and a claims experience of over 95 per cent. You don't want the cheapest plan that comes from a firm that rejects a lot of claims. Try and buy online to cut out the agent commission.

This is a frill-free product; you don't need to worry about the agent's livelihood. Most insurance companies now have systems that anyway remind you before the premium is due. Your fourth cell in the money box now has a product.

## Almost-There cell

These are investments you make for needs that are two to three years in the future. The products in this cell are similar to the ones in the emergency cell. Use either FDs, if you don't understand funds and are not willing to take on a higher risk for your short-term needs, or a money-market fund for needs up to two years. For needs within one year, use a low-risk liquid fund.

We don't want an equity fund for this cell, because equity can be volatile and we want certainty about the availability of the money. This is your fifth cell now looking good.

You can estimate your own goals by filling the worksheet on page 232.

## In-Some-Time investments

These are for needs that are three to seven years in the future. For different age groups, the goals are different. From this cell on, the use of equity becomes really important. I've explained equity in great detail earlier. It is safe if you follow the rules. Mutual funds are safer than direct stock-picking. And you have no recourse but to learn about them.

The closer your goal is to three years, the larger the proportion of safer products; and the nearer it is towards the seven-year mark, the more risk your portfolio can handle. For a goal that is three years away, you can use a mix of money market and banking and PSU debt funds.

For a goal closer to seven years, go towards conservative hybrid funds. The closer you are to the seven-years goal, the more risk you can take. For those who understand the risk, using aggressive hybrid funds is also a good idea. We're now done with the sixth cell.

You can estimate your own goals by filling the worksheet on page 236.

## Far-Away investments

These are for all goals other than retirement. Retirement has its own cell. You may be saving for your kids' education or your own house, and the goal may be more than seven years away. I am for going all the way to 100 per cent in equity mutual funds for my goals that are beyond seven years.

Within this cell, you can have a mix of more or less aggressive equity. If your goals are around the seven- to ten-year mark, go with more of aggressive hybrid mutual funds, broadmarket index and large- and mid-cap funds, and have a smaller proportion of mid-cap, small-cap and sector funds.

For goals beyond ten years, you can hike the proportion of mid- and small-cap funds. The largest part of the equity fund portfolio must remain in lower-risk mix of index funds and large- and mid-cap funds. Only if you understand funds well should you risk allocations to both mid- and small-cap funds. This was cell seven.

You can estimate your own goals by filling the worksheet on page 240.

## Retirement fund

This cell has a mix of products. The core is your PF and PPF. The rest is in equity funds. What kind of funds? The further away from retirement you are, the more risk you can take. For people in their thirties, a larger allocation to mid-, small-cap and sector funds would not hurt if chosen well. But if you are already in your late forties or early fifties, stay conservative with broadmarket index and large- and mid-cap funds.

I devote an entire chapter to how to think about the contents of this cell, which is the next one.

Eight cells are now done. But we're not through just yet.

You can estimate your own goals by filling the worksheet on page 244.

## Gold and real estate

Gold has its own cell. But it is tiny. No more than 5–10 per cent of your total portfolio is in gold, and that too paper gold, not jewellery. The government's sovereign bond issue is very good and if you don't need the money for the next seven years, you can begin to build a gold laddering system. It is useful for inflation-protection and for use in marriages of the kids.

I actually have no gold in my portfolio. I depend on well-chosen equity funds to do that for me. I'm not planning to go big on gold on my kid's wedding. So, no need for gold for me. But each family is different. If you think you'd want to gift gold to the kids at the time of their marriages, go ahead and invest. But not in jewellery; it should be either in an ETF or in gold bonds. This was cell nine. It is tiny and we don't count our gold trinkets in this cell.

Real estate has its own cell, but the only product I have in that cell is the house I own and live in. You know that I'm not a big fan of real estate. I find it really messy. Keep it down to the one house you live in. If you can manage the stress that comes with real estate, add to the cell, but do remember to look at your overall asset allocation. Real estate as investment should not be the biggest share of the net worth. We can work much better with real estate as a financial product once more real estate investment trusts or REITs come to the market, and when they do, I will probably redo this allocation. But for now, avoid. Cell ten is done.

It is not enough to create the box, you need to periodically clean it. Go to Chapter 12 to see how to redo the money box. But we are not done populating our box. There is another cell that carries your estate plan. That cell we will meet in Chapter 13.

> Choosing products is by far the most difficult part of a financial plan. Just narrowing down the product categories helps you shortlist the funds that you need to look at.
> **You are doing okay if**
>
> 1. you understand that the further away your goal, the more risk you can take;
> 2. for your near-term goals within three years, you invest in liquid and money market funds,
> 3. for your medium-term goals that are about three to seven years in the future, you invest in money market, banking and PSU bond funds and conservative hybrid funds; and
> 4. for your long-term goals that are seven or more years away, you invest in a mix of index, large- and mid-cap and small-cap funds.

# PUTTING IT ALL TOGETHER

Each product in your money box needs to fight with the others to justify its space.

## Some basic features you MUST understand

### COST
1. Cost to buy a product
2. Ongoing costs to stay in a product
3. Exit costs

### RETURN
- Compare return to an FD
- Ask for
  - Average annual returns
  - Benchmark returns
  - Category returns

### LOCK-IN
Stops you from withdrawing your money midway

### TAXES
Check:
- Does the product give you a tax break?
- Is the return tax-free?
- What is the capital gain tax?

### HOLDING PERIOD
Ask each product: How long do I need to hold it for it to work for me?

Ask seller to write down the cost-to-exit and over what time period

---

1. Set up cash flow system and online/mobile banking

2. Emergency cell
   - a) FD
   - b) Mutual funds

3. Medical insurance — read the fine print

4. Life insurance: No unit-linked insurance plans, money-back, endowment, whole life policy. Go with a term plan!

5. Almost-there: avoid pure equity

6. In-some-time: go for some equity

7. Far-away: 100% in equity mutual funds

8. Retirement fund: PF+PPF+Equity

### ASSET Allocation

A mix of assets in your portfolio reduces risk & safeguards your money from inflation

- Market hits
- Equity gives the return kicker
- Gold ADDS diversification
- Inflation
- Debt funds build a stable core

# 11

# MY RETIREMENT

> *You need to target eighteen to thirty-five times your annual spending at sixty for your retirement.*

I plan not to retire. I love what I do, and frankly, wouldn't know what to do with myself if I don't go to work every day. I know lots of people who plan to keep working till they die. This is all very good, but two things can go wrong. One, health; two, supply of work. When we're young, we underestimate the damage that an ageing body causes to work. Lifestyle diseases, bad backs, knees, neck and lower immunity cause us to reduce the work we do.

Then there is the other question of the ability to get work that pays the bills once you are past your prime. What we know and can do need upgrades over time, and as we age we find it difficult to rework what we are and gather new skills. How do we know that when we hit sixty-five or seventy or eighty, there will be a skill that can throw off an income? We need to create a retirement corpus so that by age sixty, we are financially free.

Financially free. What a ring these words have! What do these two words really mean, and do we need to wait till age sixty? *You are financially free when you don't need to work to pay your bills. You have enough assets that generate enough income today and for the rest of your life.*

Some people also call it Go-to-Hell money. This is the money that you need in your money box before you can say the three words you may have been wanting to say for a long time to your boss.

You actually don't need to wait till you are sixty to get to that number. I knew a young guy once many, many years ago, who, at age twenty-eight, was convinced that all he needed was Rs 1 crore. And then what, I would ask? 'Then I will chill,' he would say.

Chill. Nice word. But unpack it a bit and you find that unless there is some purpose to your daily life, even chilling is boring. The romantic dream of having a cottage in the mountains, or by the sea, and 'pottering' about all day is – for the want of a better word – unreal.

Gosh, I would get bored in a few weeks of doing nothing. Studies show that having meaning in work ranks way above money to most people. And this is one life – why waste it in just 'chilling'? The guy is now greyer, wiser, and goes to work each day even though he does not need to.

But having enough money to retire gives you many freedoms. Freedom to choose the work you want to do, when you want to do it, and how much you want to do. I'm not talking of the super wealthy who can hire jets or zip off to watch a match abroad at a moment's notice. But regular folk like you and me. We have lifestyle expenses, but our basic middle-class background keeps a lid on most of these.

So, I'm not going to bore you with the same old arguments of how your kids won't look after you, so prepare for your own retirement. If you've been a good parent, your kids will look after you. Even if you haven't, most kids will still look after their parents.

The idea of financial freedom is to be free of any strings. Either from the boss or from your kids when you are old. This chapter is about finding out how much is enough. We know that we need a large amount of money in the future because of inflation. But exactly how big is big?

I use two rules of thumb to get to a rough estimate of how much is enough. These are rules of thumb, which mean that these are not exact numbers but a general estimate. Each person who reads this will need to bump this number up or down keeping their unique situation in mind.

The first one uses your current income which I call 'Save Your Age'. The second one – 'Multiply Your Spend' – uses your current expenditure to forecast what you will need in the future and how much you need to have.

There are just too many things that change in thirty years. We cannot imagine what prices, expenses and our own wants will be over that expanse of time. Did we know twenty years ago that every three years we'd be spending a small fortune on a hand-held gadget that also makes calls? Did we know that other than groceries and fuel, broadband cost will be part of the monthly family expense? And did we ever imagine that the Rs 50 we paid for a doctor's consultancy fee two decades away will balloon to Rs 1,500 in a five-star corporate hospital?

Inflation is relentless, and even when the rate of inflation falls it does not mean that prices go down. They just rise more slowly. Getting the right amount for retirement is a tough nut to crack. Targeting too large a number, making compromises on lifestyle today, and having too little is not something we want to think about. So how much is enough?

While most of the Western models look at a retirement corpus that will go to zero at age ninety or ninety-nine (people will keep eating into the capital till they either die or run out of money), this will not work in India.

From all the old people I know, the capital they have is sacrosanct. The last thing they will do is have a plan that draws down on the capital. The capital will be left as inheritance to the kids, along with the house and other assets. Given our own cultural background, how do we plan for our retirements? How do we know that we're on track?

## Save your age

At age twenty-five, save 25 per cent of your post-tax income, at age thirty, save 30 per cent of your post-tax income. At age forty save 40 per cent. This formula works if you don't have a single rupee saved towards your retirement, till you are forty. For example, if you are forty years old and have not a rupee of provident fund or real estate or gold or mutual funds, then you need to be saving very hard and will need to save 40 per cent of your post-tax income for your retirement. If your take-home pay is Rs 1 lakh a month, you are saving Rs 40,000 a month at age forty, but if you are thirty years old, you are saving only Rs 30,000. Notice how the saving ratio reduces with age – the younger you are, the less you need to save.

There is complicated maths behind these easy numbers that I am leaving out here. These are dealt with in the Appendix chapter.

But you're asking: What happens after age forty? If our goal is to retire at age sixty, the time left for savings to do their work gets reduced and you have to pull harder at the savings rate. By age fifty, if you really have not a single rupee saved, you must salt away 80 per cent of your post-tax income.

It is almost too late at fifty to save for retirement if you have nothing in the retirement kitty at all. But most of us do have something and it is good to add those numbers up to see what you have before you begin a big panic attack.

## Multiply your spend

A better way to target a retirement number is to look at your current expenditure each month and each year. An expense multiplier is, in fact, a better way to crack the same problem, because at the same level of income, different families will have very different spending behaviour.

I know families that don't know where their money goes and others who have tiny expenses because of their chosen lifestyle. An expense multiplier assumes that you know how much you spend, but many families are clueless of their annual expense number – money comes in and money goes out.

If you have got your cash flows in place, you know your current annual expenses. Your first step is to use a simple future value calculator to see how much you will need today. For example, if your current annual expense is Rs 6 lakhs at age thirty, and we assume an inflation of 6 per cent, in thirty years, at age sixty, you will need Rs 34.46 lakhs a year.

You'll need 70 per cent of your last working year expense in your first non-working year. And then this expense will now grow at 6 per cent a year till you hit 100. I'm assuming you live till 100. What this means is that if you were spending Rs 1 lakh a month when you retired, your expenses will drop to Rs 70,000 a month in the first year post retirement.

This is because costs related to travel to and from work, wardrobe, entertainment, food and other such expenses reduce once you stop going to work. But your monthly expenditure does not stay at Rs 70,000 a month, it begins to creep up again due to inflation. In how many years will this Rs 70,000 double? If inflation is 6 per cent, then at age seventy-two you'll be spending Rs 1.4 lakhs a month.

Use the Rule of 72 again to do the maths. This time you divide 72 by the inflation you are projecting into the future. For example, if we think inflation will be 6 per cent in the future, divide 72 by 6. This means you will spend twice of today's expenditure in twelve years. If you spend Rs 1 lakh a month, in twelve years you will spend Rs 2 lakhs a month. In another twelve years, you will be spending Rs 4 lakhs a month; in another twelve years, you will be spending Rs 8 lakhs a month. Remember: Divide 72 with your inflation number to get the number of years it will take to double your current expenses.

Now you know how much you will spend in the first year of retirement, but what does this mean for your retirement kitty? How much will you need at retirement? *At age sixty, you need between eighteen to thirty-five times your annual expenses at retirement to retire with the lifestyle you are used to.*

For example, if you are spending an annual Rs 12 lakhs at sixty, you need a retirement corpus of at least Rs 2.2 crores to retire, if you plan to eat up all the money and leave nothing to heirs. If you want to leave the entire corpus to your children, the same annual expense will need a corpus of Rs 4.2 crores. If you plan to leave half your corpus, then you are targeting a corpus of around Rs 3 crores.

In this case you are taking a multiplier that is halfway between eighteen and thirty-five or, approximately, twenty-six. Multiply 12 lakhs with twenty-six and you get Rs 3 crores. The younger you are today, the larger will be the corpus in the future, but the multiplier remains the same. Hope this number with lots of zeros behind scares you into investing right away.

There are a lot of assumptions I've had to use to make these projections; look at 'Appendix' to see them. The future is out there and there are too many things that can change along the way. At a macro level, inflation rates could drop, growth could take off even more, resulting not only in better-than-expected increments but also better-than-expected equity returns.

The reverse could happen. At a personal level, you could do really well or really badly. You could have a healthy life or you could battle some life-threatening disease that upsets your money calculations. There is no way we can predict the future; the only thing we know is what we do today. Based on that we can make projections for what we need tomorrow.

I've assumed an inflation of 6 per cent all along, before and after your retirement. Post retirement, I use a very conservative 8 per cent return on your investment.

How should you use this rule of thumb? First, remember that this is a rule of thumb. This means that it is an approximation of what you will actually need. For instance, if you plan to work beyond sixty, the corpus needed will shrink. If you have other sources of post-retirement income, say rental income, the corpus needed is less.

## Retirement milestones

Five, ten, fifteen, twenty years – it is a long way off. We can begin on a plan, but how do we know that we are on track? If the goal is to have enough at age sixty, is there another rule of thumb that can help us map our progress as we age? Fidelity Investments has a retirement guideline out that maps the journey of the retirement corpus over the years.

*At age forty, you should have three times your annual income as your retirement corpus already.* If you earn Rs 15 lakhs a year at age forty, you should have Rs 45 lakhs in your retirement corpus. *At fifty, you should have six times your annual income.* If you have an annual income of Rs 40 lakhs at age fifty, you should already have Rs 2.4 crores in your corpus. *At age sixty, or at retirement, you should have eight times your annual salary.* Earning a crore at sixty, you must have Rs 8 crores as corpus. Remember, this assumes that you will burn through your entire retirement corpus and leave nothing as inheritance out of your retirement kitty.

The Fidelity numbers assume a US scenario with social security and other benefits, but the multipliers roughly work out to a rule of thumb for India as well.

## How to get the money

This sounds too much to do. Who can save so much in the early years and what about the other goals like kids' education, their marriage, a house and vacations? Let's open up these numbers.

First, you need to save this much only if you don't have a single rupee in savings anywhere. If you have savings or other assets, this number will come down. If you plan to keep working beyond age sixty, this number will come down. Most people have more than they think.

Consolidate your money. There will always be money lying around in savings deposits waiting for an emergency. We hoard cash thinking that we will need it in the near future. I know a family that kept Rs 7 lakhs in a saving deposit for over five years waiting for the 'sudden need'.

We learnt how to create an emergency fund, a medical cover for your family and a pure term cover for yourself to build a safety net. You need less-liquid cash if you do these three things.

Next, count all the balances in your provident fund, your public provident fund, your fixed deposits, gold, any real estate other than the home you live in. Include the value of your mutual funds if any; find out what the value of the endowment or money-back policies are and count those in as well. The more you have already, the less you need to target. Do not underestimate the power of order in your money box.

Two, remember that you are already saving 24 per cent of your basic income through your employees' provident fund (EPF) deductions. You contribute 12 per cent and your employer matches that. By age thirty, most people have begun to do at least their tax-saving investments, if not a bit more. Count that in when you think about the 30 per cent or 40 per cent number we read about in the 'Save your age' section earlier.

If you are self-employed or not part of an EPF, you are more vulnerable than those with a mandatory retirement plan in place. As the first step, make it mandatory in your head to save at least as much as others with their EPF. Then keep bumping up the number as your spending gets used to the saving rhythm.

Three, saving becomes a habit when you remove what you want to save from your spending money. Cash in the bank gets spent. And spending adjusts to what is available. Separate out what you intend to save from your salary or money-inflow account. Now you see why we got our cash flows in order?

Four, the rule of thumb can be tweaked into an easier saving schedule once you get used to saving and investing. The thirties and forties in a householder's life are the decades of high expenses: the home and car EMIs are high; kids are growing up; and you are saving for their education and marriage.

But the decade of the fifties is one of high income and much lower expenditure. You are at the peak of your earning cycle. Your home EMIs are paid off (if they are not, know that they should be). Your kids are financially independent.

This is the decade when you can save at least half your income. I know people who save almost 70 per cent of their income at this age. If you are disciplined enough to target a much higher saving rate in your fifties, you can reduce the burden on your younger self.

I've devoted an entire chapter to retirement while you may be today worrying about making a down payment on a home or about your child's education or marriage. But you need to put on your oxygen mask first. When you travel by air, you must have heard the safety instruction – in case of an emergency, put on your oxygen mask first.

You need to have an eye on your retirement corpus, even as you build funds for your kids' education and marriage. A good value system, capacity for hard work and life skills are a better bequeath than a large corpus to buy a degree from abroad. *Your oxygen mask is your retirement kitty; don't ignore that while you look after your current and more near-term money needs.*

---

This is the big goal for the future. The earlier you begin, the better it is. Small amounts can grow to big amounts if put in the right fund. Think about funding thirty-five to forty years of increasing living and medical costs after age sixty.

**You are doing okay if**

1. you are saving about 10–15 per cent of your take-home salary towards your retirement;
2. at age thirty, if you have zero retirement money, you start saving 30 per cent of your post-tax income; at age forty, 40 per cent; and at age fifty, 80 per cent of your income;
3. you are targeting a retirement kitty that is between eighteen and thirty-five times your annual spending at age sixty; and
4. by age forty, you have three times your annual income as a retirement kitty, by age fifty, six times your annual income and by age sixty, eight times your annual income as your retirement kitty.

# RETIREMENT

"Who said I'll retire? I love my work!"

Two things that can go wrong with this:
- Health
- Supply of work

**So plan for 'Financial Freedom'**

### Freedom to choose:
- **WHAT** work you want to do
- **WHEN** you want to do it
- **HOW** much you want to do

## MULTIPLY YOUR SPENDS!!

1. Calculate your current annual spend
2. Inflation-adjust to what you would spend at age 60
3. Take that number and multiply by 26!
4. Yup, it's a very large number
5. Start planning at once!

How much is enough? 10 crore?

### Retirement Milestones

| Age 40 | Age 50 | Retirement at 60 |
| --- | --- | --- |
| 3X annual income | 6X annual income | 8X annual income |

### How to get the money?

1. Start with a monthly investment plan
2. Be regular
3. Use an index fund
4. Save more as you grow older

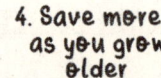

## 12

# REDO THE BOX

*The 'fill it, shut it, forget it' approach needs a once-in-a-year audit. Your situation may change or the products may get better or worse. Once a year is often enough to clean your money box.*

When I began constructing my own money box, it took me almost 6–8 months to get the cash-flow banks in place. And then a few years later I had to redo parts of the system once again. Our financial lives are messy. Too many bank accounts, joint accounts with spouse, parents, kids. But once done, the work has still not finished. Stuff happens. You lose jobs, you change them, you move cities, kids get independent, you can lose a spouse or get a divorce, parents die – plenty of stuff can happen to your money box.

But the structure you create always gives you a framework to return to, once the tornado of life events passes by. In my case, my husband moved to a new job in a different city and we had to rework the bank accounts. Getting the cash-flow system right is key to the whole money box working smoothly.

Of course, you need to use online banking to move money between accounts and into products to make this work smoothly. Setting up again the life, medical and emergency fund will take time; choosing and then setting up the SIPs will take time. But once all this legwork is done, you really have the luxury of knowing that your money is working to a plan and you don't need to think every few months 'now what to buy'.

Not just our lives, but the products on sale are also dynamic. Sometimes a better product comes along and you may need to switch out of what you have into the new one, if the costs of the transition are small. For example, the government's sovereign gold bond issues are the best way to hold gold today. They are better than the ETF route since there is no cost and you get a nominal interest on your gold holding. Or when term life insurance plans went online around the year 2010, the premiums crashed to almost half, since the agent commission was removed from a direct sale. We dumped our older plans and bought new ones, despite the fact that at an older age bracket we had to pay more premiums.

Your money box is a dynamic entity and it needs periodic checks to see if your situation has changed, or there are better products on offer.

## What to do when you change

Change can come in many ways. The most unstoppable one is age. The composition of your money box changes as you age. For example, as you near retirement and your retirement corpus builds up, your kids become independent, the need for a life insurance policy goes away. We only need a life cover if the family depends on your monthly pay cheque. Once you have your retirement corpus in place, and are free from loans, you don't need a life cover.

If you are sitting on a really cheap term plan from your thirties, there is no harm in continuing with it, but you need not top up or buy more. As you age, your risk capacity reduces, and it is a good idea to rework your asset allocation, reducing equity as you age.

There is a rule of thumb on how much equity you should hold: 100 minus your age. At age thirty, you should have 70 per cent of your holdings in equity and at age seventy, you should have 30 per cent of your holdings in equity. It is a good idea to do an annual audit of your money box to see if you are on track.

Personal changes could be around jobs. You could move to a much higher-paying job or your partner could go to work causing the family income to rise. Your risk capacity increases as more money flows into the money box. Remember to use it not just to hike lifestyle but also the savings. Your kids could grow up and become independent, freeing up funds as the goals for their education and marriage are met.

The Invest-It box can really get to work for your retirement with all this money that now gets diverted from the education and marriage fund to your retirement fund. You could inherit a bunch of money or assets from your parents. That infusion will again need to realign your money box.

## What to do when products change

You should replace a product from your money box with a new one in the market only if it is a better product in itself, or the replacement is made necessary due to changes in your circumstances. *A better product is either cheaper or gives better benefits, or both*.

If you invest in managed funds, and not ETFs and index funds, you need to check if the funds you have chosen are still good. Sometimes fund houses lose steam, they get sold, fund managers leave, or have a series of bad years. Managed funds mean that you have to track the funds in your money box. If the funds no longer make the cut, it is better to redeem and switch to other funds. If you don't see yourself doing all this, stay with ETFs or index funds.

## Should you redo your box when markets rise or fall?

Rising too hard, or falling too fast – most of us get influenced by the herd mentality and want to sell when the stock markets are crashing and want to buy more when they are rising. I recently got a mail from a family friend who wanted to invest some money for his father, sisters and himself. He works with a planner who had recommended hybrid mutual funds, given the profile of the people and the sharp rise of markets beyond valuation at that point. It was a lump-sum investment and the planner, rightly, did not want his client to take home the risk of a sudden drop in prices immediately post investment.

My friend wrote to me to say that his family wanted to take more risk than what the planner was recommending, and asked what he should do. Rising markets have the effect of making people take more risk than they should. My advice to my friend was to stay with the planner's recommendations and stay grounded with a more conservative portfolio, given the age and state of the family.

You must redo your box, but in the opposite direction of the market movement. A rising market changes the nature of the asset allocation you said you were comfortable with. If the thought of 50:50 allocation in equity and debt looked good to you when markets were low, why should that change when markets are high?

If the rise in markets changes your allocation ratio to 60:40, you need to rebalance; that is, sell equity and buy more debt funds or bonds to go back to the 50:50 allocation. In falling markets, the opposite is true. Why will you sell when the price is down? That's the time to buy more to get your allocation back to the level you said you wanted. Be careful that market frenzies and sulks don't sweep you off your feet.

***It is usually a good idea to open the box once a year to evaluate if it needs a change.*** If you have managed funds, it is a good idea to check twice a year that your products are on course. If you are an index-fund or ETF person, you don't need more than an annual check. That, remember, is the purpose of this book. To free your time and mind from worrying about financial security to do more meaningful things.

> Things change – you get older, personal situations change, the economic environment changes, the financial products change. You need to look at your money box again to keep it up to date with all these changes.
>
> **You are doing okay if**
>
> 1. you don't watch the stock market tickers and then change your money box;
> 2. you set up dates twice a year to redo your money box (attaching them to major festivals or birthdays that are about six months apart being a good nudge);
> 3. you rebalance your portfolio and return to your asset allocation, which means sometimes selling some equity when a bull run is raging; and
> 4. a personal situation changes and you reconfigure the box accordingly to suit the change.

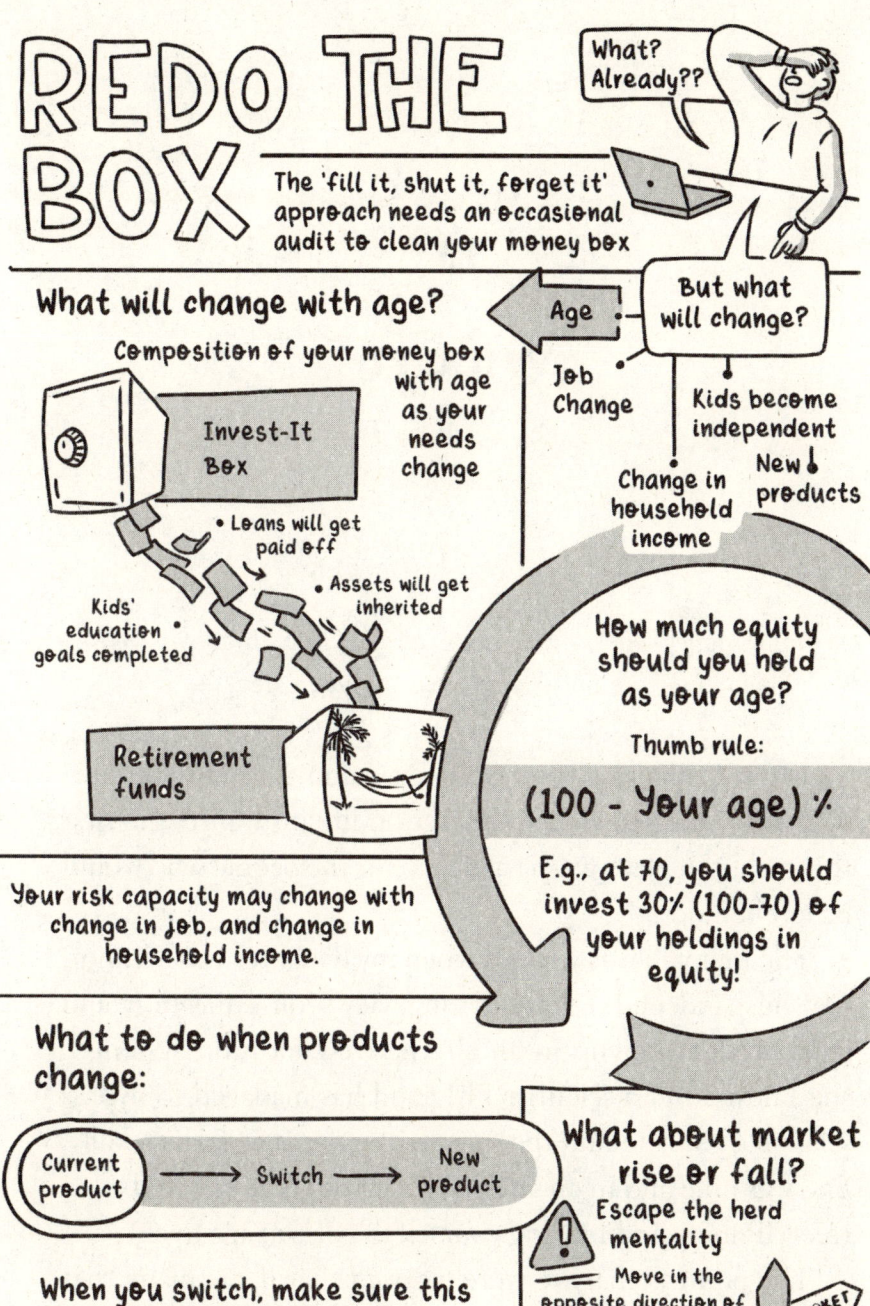

# 13

# WILL IT

*Your money box is half done till you have made a will. Nominations are not enough. Will it if you care.*

After I did the 'shut-your-eyes-and-imagine-you-are-dead' exercise in the chapter on life insurance, the first thing I put in place was a road map for the people who would be left behind.

The first will was written when my daughter was a minor. My husband and I have strong views on education and have brought her up in an alternative education system – she's now a brain scientist PhD and has managed to bypass Class 10, Class 12 and the university system in India totally. She was nine and in an alternative school that had wall- and tree-climbing and feeding yourself as goals at age five.

The point is that we were worried that if the plane that had us both in its belly went down, what'd happen to her and our way of life that she was used to? We decided to appoint two legal guardians who understood what we wanted. Wrote extensive details in the will. The important thing was to tell her about this – but do kids of nine even worry about stuff like that?

It seems they do. I spoke to her once when we were out junk-fooding – 'Do you worry about being left alone?' After a twenty-second pause, she nodded. A parent of a student in her class had died and the thought that both her parents could die was certainly there in her head. So I told her about the will, told her who the guardians were, told her where the document was kept.

I told her that there would be enough through insurance covers for her future. Growing up in a financially aware household like ours, she knew the basics already and tucked away the information and got right back to the shake and the pizza. Luckily for all of us, that will was never used. A new one has taken its place now that she is no longer a minor.

Not making a will reflects the biggest wonder of this world – we see people dying all around us; yet we believe that we are immortal. Some people consider it bad luck, some think you are tempting fate, and others just are convinced that they will not die anytime soon.

Whatever your reason, understand the fact that *not making a will will tick the 'most-selfish-thing-I've-ever-done' box in my book.* You're leaving behind a mess for your family, especially if there are joint assets with an extended family or you have created assets with your parents, making your siblings an heir to the property you thought you were leaving to your kids. Let's get some basic myths out of the way.

## Why make a will, my assets will go to my family

If you die without a will, your house, gold, car, mutual funds, jewellery will go to your legal heirs. Who the legal heirs are depends on your religion in India and which personal law applies to you. For example, if you are a Hindu, and die intestate (without a will), your assets will be divided equally among Class I heirs. There is a list of twelve relations that fall in this category, including sons, daughters, surviving spouse and mother.

Things get complicated when there are joint assets in the extended family, especially in real estate. Just writing down how you want your assets to be distributed solves a lot of the post-death trauma to the family. Second-guessing what you wanted to do after you are gone is an unfair burden you place on your family.

## Why make a will, my kids won't fight over my assets

There was a man who said this. He had two sons and a daughter. All very erudite and genteel. And no, they did not fight at all after the man passed away after a long and meaningful life. But it was a nightmare for the kids, sorting his estate out – just getting the documentation done to transfer assets took time and effort. Things become even tougher if the kids are not in India any more. You may have really great kids, and they may not fight over the assets, but it is just unkind not to leave a road map for them. In fact, NRI kids are now requesting their parents in India to please sell their real estate investments rather than leave a mess behind.

## Why make a will, I have nominations in place

A common enough pushback to a will. But did you know that a nomination does not mean that the nominees get the assets? Look at the nominee as a caretaker of the asset, somebody to whom the money flows for safekeeping till the legal heirs can stake a claim. In your head the nominee and the legal heir is the same person, but in the eyes of the law, the two could be different.

## How to make a will

You'll have to map the current assets – bank deposits, bonds, mutual funds, stocks, properties, gold, jewellery, vehicles, assets created overseas, books, art, wine and whatever you want to bequeath to your heirs. It's a good idea to make an itemized list of things: where they are kept and where the papers that establish the claim are kept.

It's always a good idea to put down details like passwords to online bank accounts in a diary that you keep under lock and key. Put down in writing the location of property papers and locker keys.

Once the details are done, indicate who should get what. For example, if you have two flats and want to leave one to each kid, do specify which one goes to whom. If there is jewellery, mention who gets what. Maybe take pictures and specify who gets what. Don't forget to include ownership of social media accounts, email addresses, intellectual property rights.

The myth of a big happy family gets destroyed at some point in most people's lives. So do your kids and surviving spouse a favour and pin down details of what you want to do with your assets. A couple should make individual wills and not a joint will.

What if you want to leave unequal bequests? Maybe one of the two kids has been more supportive to you in your old age. Will the prodigal child contest your unequal will? Probably. To prevent that, you can include what is called an 'in terrorem' clause. This is usually put in a will when a contest of the will is anticipated. This means that if any of the beneficiaries contest the will, they could lose even what has been bequeathed to them.

Next, you need to appoint an executor of the will. Ideally the beneficiary of the will is not the executor. This could be a family friend, your lawyer, your financial planner who ensures that the will is followed in letter and spirit in the asset distribution. You can write a will on a piece of paper, sign it with a date and place, and get two witnesses to sign as well. The witness and the beneficiary should be different people, and the witness and the executor should be younger than you. Do simple things like numbering each page, signing each page and putting down the date clearly.

## The toughest talk ever

I remember speaking to an old friend. The conversation veered around to ageing parents, and he confessed to the difficulty in talking to his eighty-year-old father about end-of-life choices, putting his assets in order and writing a will. Over the past decade and a half, he says, he's been through various stages – indifference (this will sort itself out), denial (my old man won't cop it so soon), guilt (what am I doing thinking about the death of my own folk?), worry (gosh, the run-around XYZ went through to get basic bank accounts unfrozen, and don't even talk about the real estate mess), then courage (I'm going to nail this talk next time we meet) and finally to despair (Dad doesn't want to discuss it!).

It's not the easiest thing to discuss your ageing parents' financial affairs and asking them if they have thought about making a will and having a larger plan in mind about the transition into the other world and the care of the spouse who and assets that would be left behind. A chunk of the forty-plus urban mass affluent Indians are watching their parents age – slowly but incrementally.

For this slice of the Indian population, whom I like to call the urban professional mass affluent, dealing with this transition is breaking new territory where there are no old rules of tradition and precedence to fall back upon. Around thirty to forty years ago the norm was (and continues to be in smaller towns and rural India) that ageing parents were looked after by their eldest son, and because the families mostly lived together, the transition from one generation to the other was gradual. Slowly the younger family member would take over the various tasks of running the house and finances – so things like location of documents, names on bank accounts and location of locker keys weren't such an issue. Usually the sisters' dowries took care of their inheritance issues (most signed over their rights to the brothers) and the brothers would sort out the family assets the best they could.

But for the urban professional mass affluent Indian born post Independence, the story is very different. The parents mostly continue to lead independent lives, with assistance now and then, and very little intervention in the day-to-day running of the house or finances.

However, smoothening the end-of-life issues needs more attention than ever before. In the generations gone by, the focus was on care and who would provide it, but for the current set of urban oldies, the concerns are more about lifestyle, independence and space. Issues to be sorted out are end-of-life choices, the continuation of the accustomed life for the spouse left behind, paperwork, bequeathing real assets and closure of debts.

But my dipstick survey among people like us tells me that this conversation jostles with the 'birds and the bees' talk with the kids in terms of the squeamishness.

What makes the conversation on end-of-life choices tough to initiate is also the fear of appearing overeager to discuss your own inheritance. Professors Marsha A. Goetting and Vicki L. Schmall in Montana State University Guide write:

> Sometimes people hesitate to discuss financial concerns with their parents for fear of appearing overly interested in their inheritances. After all, talking about passing on Mom and Dad's money usually means talking about the circumstances under which it will be transferred. Few of us want to start a conversation with, 'Dad, when you die' ... or 'Mom, if you become unable to make decisions' ...

From the parents' point of view as well, it is difficult to think about your own mortality, and the inter-generational transfer of assets is many times fraught with undercurrents of tension.

Will the child who supports me more stop the care if I divide assets equally? What if I want to leave all my things to the faith-based organization I belong to? Will this be an issue with the children?

For both sets of people across the generation divide, it may be easier to begin the conversation by either discussing the story of somebody else, who did or did not put affairs in order before moving on, or getting a trusted family friend to help initiate it.

Beyond the basic registered will document, the conversation needs to move on to end-of-life choices. A friend's mother was sure she did not want to look into the eyes of the ventilator when she breathed her last. That choice was respected when the time came.

It is important for you to have that conversation. If the topic is fraught with landmines of emotion, guilt and past family baggage, involve a trusted family friend or a financial planner. I've noticed that the people who are working with planners are able to deal with this much better than those without. (I've sourced parts of this piece from a column I wrote for *Mint* in August 2013.)

Complete your money box with a will in the final cell of the box. Hope that it is opened only after you die of old age and not before.

---

Life is fragile. Life is tenacious. We really don't know if the next day will come or not. Unclaimed investments and life insurance money run into thousands of crores.

**You are doing okay if**

1. you have a valid will in place no matter what your age and stage (it's okay to have a will at age thirty-five);
2. your will has details of all the assets and details about who gets what;
3. you have informed your family about the existence and location of the will; and
4. you have made a plan for your family to use the proceeds of the insurance policies and assets to smoothen their transition.

# WILL IT!

Making a will is like leaving a roadmap for your loved ones.

## WHY PEOPLE DON'T MAKE A WILL?

 **MY ASSETS WILL GO TO MY FAMILY**

Without a will, your assets go to your LEGAL HEIRS, which depend on your religion and what personal law applies to you. Joint assets with extended family add to the complications.

**2 MY KIDS WON'T FIGHT OVER MY ASSETS**

Sorting assets out, getting the documentation done & transferring assets takes time & effort. Making a roadmap for your kids, especially if they live in a different city/country, makes their life EASY.

 **I HAVE NOMINATIONS IN PLACE**

Nominee may not mean the same as LEGAL HEIR in the eyes of the law. A nominee is a caretaker of assets, to whom the money flows for safekeeping till the legal heir can take claim.

## HOW TO MAKE A WILL?

1. Make an itemized list of all your assets & where the documents are kept.

2. Make a protected dynamic Excel sheet with all important passwords, location of keys and property papers.

3. Indicate who gets what. (Include social media, intellectual property, etc.)

4. Make individual wills, not a combined one with your spouse.

5. Appoint an executor & get two witnesses for the will.

6. You and the witnesses sign all pages with the date.

## HAVE THE TOUGHEST TALK EVER:

It's not easy to talk to your parents about their plans on making a will but it needs to be done.

Where did we fall short in loving our kids??

- **INVOLVE A TRUSTED FAMILY FRIEND OR FINANCIAL PLANNER**
- Start with an example of someone who left without a will and how that affected the family!

**COMPLETE YOUR MONEY BOX WITH A WILL IN THE FINAL CELL**

# 14

# WHAT KILLS A MONEY BOX?

*Buying without a thought, borrowing money you can't pay back and greed are enemies of your money box.*

Other than accidents, death, divorce and job loss, there is another danger that lurks around your money box. You can't buy an insurance cover against it and you can't blame others for it. It is easy to point a finger at others to complain about the poor outcomes of financial products, but a look in the mirror may see that finger pointing right back at us. We can be the biggest enemies of our own money box.

## Spending too much

You've sweated it out in school and in university to get that job. This is meant to be 'your' time, when you are young and beautiful, and the luxury of time stretches out endlessly. Old age happens to your parents and not to you. There is the peer pressure to look good, buy the brands, hang out in all the cool places and go for exotic holidays.

All this needs money. There is the rent, the living costs, the car that must match your dreams. Money, money, money. Spending beyond what you can afford is a sure way to break your money box. And the thing about money is this – unless locked down, it gets spent. I've experienced this myself – no matter how much I withdraw from the ATM, the money disappears in a week or ten days.

Cash still hurts to pull out and use, but a UPI app, a card, or an e-wallet is smooth. What is even more smooth is the credit card. This is money you don't have. You are borrowing to spend. And as long as you keep paying back before the last date, you are good, but if you begin to fall behind on payments, the possibility of getting into a debt trap are very real.

I was teaching a bunch of budding business journalists at the Asian College of Journalism in Chennai in 2017 and I asked what the cost of default on a credit card payment is. One person raised his hand and said it cost about 18 per cent. Do you know how much interest you pay if you don't pay your card bill on time? It can vary between 24 per cent and 48 per cent. Do you remember what your savings deposit gives you? Less than 3 per cent. Your FD gives you between 4.5 and 5.5 per cent return, a debt fund about 6–8 per cent, and equity fund about 12–15 per cent (over the long term). It is better to pay off your high-cost debt than save.

Most of us clean up our spending act by the time we get married and a kid comes along. For most people, the birth of a child is that sobering moment after which the relationship with money changes for good. But is there a way to be young and restless and yet not destroy your money box?

Yes, there is. Use the cash-flow system I described earlier to start saving a bit of money. Don't wait for the time when you have money to save. You never will. Nobody ever has 'enough' money to start saving. Save a thousand bucks if you can, but make a start. The other thing to do is to begin making choices between need and greed. When you walk into the mall, the stuff on display, the smells, the lights, the sounds, the whole energy is screaming: spend, spend, spend.

You are too fat or thin, you are too dark or white, you are too tall or short, you are just not good enough till you have bought this stuff. Take a moment to think why you need something – do you need ten wristwatches? Is there space in the cupboard for that new dress? Or in the shoe rack?

I remember meeting this woman doctor in the US once. I was spending a semester at Yale, New Haven, and she was visiting. We got talking and the conversation veered to shopping. She said that she and her husband (there were no kids) had just moved to a bigger home because the stuff they had needed more space. She said that she had more than twenty pairs of boots but ended up wearing just one of them because that was the most comfortable. Why buy, I asked? After two or three pairs, why do you need another one? 'Because I don't have *that* one,' she said.

At some point in our lives, we need to step back to see why we're doing what we are doing. I know peer pressure kills, but whatever you do, there will always be something that you don't have. Better to be who you are rather than be somebody that you are not.

I doubt that any of us looks at ourselves and says: 'I'm greedy.' But a look at many portfolio choices taken by many people does look like greed to me. What is greed in investing? It is the desire to get rich overnight, riding a boom time in some investment. It is the desire to get rich quickly without doing too much work.

Those of you who invested in Hoffland Finance, in emu farming, in Home Trade, in other multilevel marketing (MLM) schemes that promised super returns for very little effort know what I'm talking about. The sales pitch of such products is very clear – double or triple your money in a very short time.

Such deals usually work for those who enter in the beginning of the game – later investor money is recycled to pay super returns to older investors. But at some point, when new investors stop coming, the whole pyramid collapses. The Saradha scam was one such ponzi scheme.

Other than MLM schemes, greed gets us to invest in very high-risk products – such as stock IPOs (initial public offers). I remember a relative who was a zero-risk FD investor in small-town India. One visit many years ago to his house resulted in him confessing that he had invested in the

Reliance Power IPO. He had broken his FDs and invested in it. Those who remember that IPO know that the project was not going to show returns for a very, very long time.

There was nothing in the project to justify the huge premium the IPO was charging. It was a lot of hype and had been the outcome of very high commissions paid to brokers to sell the IPO. 'Why would you buy this, when every time I tell you to invest in mutual funds, you say you can't take the risk?'

With a lot of confidence, he replied: 'The money will double in three years and if it does not, I'll go long term.' Silence in the room. I don't know where to go and bang my head. Many other financial planners and people in the financial sector agree with me that the most difficult to convince about sensible investing are your own family and extended family members.

I met the owner of a very popular fintech platform sometime back and he was traumatized that his cousin was investing in ICOs. ICO? What's that? This is an Initial Coin Offer and this story is linked to the exponential rise of bitcoin some years back. You have to be living in a cave to have escaped hearing about bitcoins and what fantastic returns they have given.

By one calculation, Rs 1 lakh invested in 2010 was worth Rs 100 crore in 2018. Some people have overnight become really rich by buying bitcoins in the last few years. A bitcoin is one kind of cryptocurrency. What this means very simply is that, unlike physical currencies like the dollar or the rupee, no government issues cryptocurrency. There is no sovereign promise to pay the bearer a sum printed on the note, as we see on rupee notes. Very simply, cryptocurrency is a programme that is not owned or controlled by one person or state, but is generated by a computer program.

Sounds so weird, right? But then why is bitcoin price zooming? If we step back and think about currencies that we use, we will realize that anything that becomes a common medium of exchange is a store of value and can become a currency. We don't know yet if bitcoins will become a global standard currency in the future, but what we do know is that bitcoin transactions are legal in some countries, have been banned in others and, in some like the US, are taxed, thus giving it legitimacy.

What does this mean for you and me? Do we buy bitcoins? I have a golden rule that has saved me money, and may have lost me lots of unrealized profits as well. *I don't invest in things I do not understand.* I don't fully understand what is giving bitcoins its value. If the argument is that it is limited in quantity, and, therefore, its value will continue to rise, I only have to look at gold and real estate prices to see where that argument goes. But the need for a global currency that smashes the monopoly of banks in money transfer has long been felt. But whether bitcoins will be that system that makes the breakthrough globally is not so clear.

But bitcoins have given super returns, how can you say that they are not good investments? My answer to this question asked by a colleague is another question: How certain are you of a Sensex-based ETF of giving inflation-plus returns if held for at least 7–10 years? Very certain, she said. How certain are you that bitcoin will give you the same return, if not more? Not certain at all.

It could make her very rich or that investment may go to zero. Bitcoin is a very high-risk product; and therefore potentially high-return investment today. Buy at your own risk and then only small quantities. *If you are not investing in mutual funds because of the risk, you are totally nuts to be investing in bitcoin.* It's like a person scared of the water, and refusing to get in the shallow, seeing a golden goose in the deep end and jumping in. You may catch the goose, and it may fly away with you and you may live happily ever after, or you may see the bottom of the pool up close.

So what are ICOs? These are people launching new cryptocurrency and hoping that it becomes the next bitcoin. Two words for you: Stay away. But if the itch of greed is too much, take 1 per cent or 2 per cent of your annual investment amount and buy bitcoins. This takes care of the urge to be a part of this phenomenon and keeps the bulk of your money safe. I'm not even doing that. Because this behaviour clashes with my other golden rule about money: if a deal is too good to be true, it is too good to be true.

Notice that I used the word 'traumatized' in an earlier para. Financial planners and advisers who care about their profession find it traumatizing to see people fall into traps and lose their money. It is like a person who knows where landmines are in the ground and is shouting to keep people off the danger zones. Those who venture ahead do get their money boxes blown apart. And here's the thing with money mistakes – when they realize they've been had, they become 'long-term' investors!

Spending too much, borrowing to spend and impulsive investment punts have the power to derail years of work on a money box. The mantra is balance, and don't lose it.

> Fear, greed and sudden knee-jerk actions have the potential to derail your carefully constructed money box.
> **You are doing okay if**
>
> 1. your spending is in control and you are paying off your credit card bills in full as they arrive each month;
> 2. your borrowing is under control with 'good' loans, like a home loan, rather than personal loans to fund lifestyle-related consumption;
> 3. you stay away from the periodic investment manias like bitcoin or emu farms; and
> 4. you continue your SIPs even if markets tank.

# WHAT KILLS A MONEY BOX?

- Divorce
- Job loss
- Accidents/Deaths

Spending more than what you can afford is a sure way to break your money box

You!
↳ Bad spending habits
↳ Buying out of peer pressure
↳ Borrowing money to pay credit card bills

Are enemies of your money box.

## How to save?

**1** **Save first, spend later**

Have a cash-flow system & follow it. You cannot wait to have enough to start saving. Start small, but start saving

**2** **Understand what's a need & what's a greed!**

**Money gets spent unless locked down**

**Do not invest in things you do not understand!**

Bitcoin & crypto seem very interesting & tempting, but don't put your heard-earned money into something you do not understand. These are VERY high-risk unregulated products.

# WORKSHEETS

## 1: THE CASH-FLOW SYSTEM WORKSHEET

Set up your cash-flow system, as described in Chapter 2, to get a clear oversight of your spending and saving.

### Sample cash-flow system

The following sample is a six-month cash-flow statement for a person with an assumed income of Rs 17.26 lakh a year. Inflows to the Income Account can differ month to month due to a bonus or a matured investment, or income from any other source. The monthly take-home income is Rs 1.25 lakh, but in Month 2 and Month 5, there is extra income. Likewise, the Spend-It Account can change too. This person decided to spend all the extra income in Month 2, but saved some of the extra income in Month 5. However, the base-level expenditure each month of Rs 85,000 remains unchanged. The Invest-It Account gets a minimum amount of Rs 40,000 a month that can go up in the months there is extra saving. This clearly gives a line of sight as to how much monthly savings can be committed to a regular investment plan.

| SAMPLE CASH-FLOW SYSTEM (Rs) | | | | | | |
|---|---|---|---|---|---|---|
| MONTH / ACCOUNT | Month 1 | Month 2 | Month 3 | Month 4 | Month 5 | Month 6 |
| Income Account | 1,25,000 | 1,40,000 | 1,25,000 | 1,25,000 | 2,23,000 | 1,25,000 |
| Spend-It Account | 85,000 | 1,00,000 | 85,000 | 85,000 | 1,50,000 | 85,000 |
| Invest-It Account | 40,000 | 40,000 | 40,000 | 40,000 | 73,000 | 40,000 |

## Your data

Now fill your own data in the following sheet. Take this as a practice session for six months where you figure out your own money flows. It is a good idea to overestimate spending and underestimate saving just so that you don't run out of money mid-month.

## YOUR CASH-FLOW SYSTEM (Rs)

| ACCOUNT / MONTH | Month 1 | Month 2 | Month 3 | Month 4 | Month 5 | Month 6 |
|---|---|---|---|---|---|---|
| Income Account | | | | | | |
| Spend-It Account | | | | | | |
| Invest-It Account | | | | | | |

## 2: THE EMERGENCY FUND WORKSHEET

Set up your emergency fund as described in Chapter 3 to get a clear oversight of how much you need to save for contingencies.

### Sample emergency fund

A good emergency fund needs at least six months of expenses in a safe place that is easy to access, typically a fixed deposit or a debt fund.

This is a sample emergency fund calculation. Six months of monthly spends in a safe place is usually enough as an emergency fund, but there can be situations where you might want to keep a larger reserve. The following numbers use the Rs 85,000 monthly base-level expense from the cash-flow sheet. Then it multiplies Rs 85,000 by the number of months you are comfortable with—six, eight, ten or twelve. Most people would be satisfied with six months, or Rs 5.1 lakh, in their emergency fund for their monthly expenses in case of need.

### SAMPLE EMERGENCY FUND ESTIMATION (Rs)

| Amount \ Months | No. of months of spending you feel safe with | 6 MONTHS | 8 MONTHS | 10 MONTHS | 12 MONTHS |
|---|---|---|---|---|---|
| Monthly Spends | 85,000 | 85,000 X 6 | 85,000 X 8 | 85,000 X 10 | 85,000 X 12 |
| Amount in the Emergency Fund | – | 5,10,000 | 6,80,000 | 8,50,000 | 10,20,000 |

## Your data

Now you put your numbers in. Pick the value of your base-level monthly expense from your own cash-flow sheet. Next decide how many months of safe money you need to target. Then multiply your monthly expense with the number of months you are comfortable with, fill the sheet and see the face of the money you need in your emergency fund.

### YOUR EMERGENCY FUND ESTIMATION (Rs)

| Amount \ Months | No. of months of spending you feel safe with | 6 MONTHS | 8 MONTHS | 10 MONTHS | 12 MONTHS |
|---|---|---|---|---|---|
| Monthly Spends | | | | | |
| Amount in the Emergency Fund | | | | | |

## 3: THE LIFE INSURANCE WORKSHEET

The need for a life insurance cover changes with age, income and the assets already created. This worksheet gives a rule-of-thumb approach to get you closer to the number that you will personally need. The larger is the existing asset base, the lower is the need for an insurance cover. In your thirties, you have few assets, hence the need for twenty-five times of annual income number for a life insurance cover. By age forty, some assets are built, but incomes are higher as well, therefore a multiple of fifteen is used. At age fifty, you are nearing retirement, and your retirement corpus should be nearing completion, therefore a multiple of ten times of annual income is used.

### Sample life insurance cover

In the following sample, three age cohorts are used to show the calculations needed. In the thirties, a person with an annual income of Rs 17 lakh, as used in the example earlier, will need a life insurance cover that is twenty-five times this number, or Rs 4.25 crore.

At age forty, a person earning an assumed Rs 30 lakh annual income will have some assets built, causing the multiplier to go down to fifteen times the annual income, or Rs 4.5 crore.

At age fifty, a person should have the retirement corpus well in place and will need a multiple of just ten to target a good cover. For a person earning an assumed Rs 50 lakh, a cover of Rs 5 crore is good enough.

| SAMPLE LIFE INSURANCE WORKSHEET (Rs lakh) | | | | |
|---|---|---|---|---|
| AGE | INSURANCE COVER MULTIPLIER | ANNUAL INCOME | INSURANCE MULTIPLIER | INSURANCE COVER NEEDED |
| In your 30s | 25 times your annual income | 17 | 17 X 25 | 425 |
| In your 40s | 15 times your annual income | 30 | 30 X 15 | 450 |
| In your 50s | 10 times your annual income | 50 | 50 X 10 | 500 |

## Your data

Plug in your own numbers in the following worksheet to see how much life cover you will need. You can get your annual income number either from your tax statement or your cash-flow statement in Worksheet 1. Remember that you must buy only a pure term cover and not a bundled life and investment policy.

| YOUR LIFE INSURANCE WORKSHEET (Rs lakh) ||||||
|---|---|---|---|---|
| AGE | INSURANCE COVER MULTIPLIER | ANNUAL INCOME | INSURANCE MULTIPLIER | INSURANCE COVER NEEDED |
| In your 30s | 25 times your annual income | | | |
| In your 40s | 15 times your annual income | | | |
| In your 50s | 10 times your annual income | | | |

# 4: COMPOUNDING TABLE

The compounding table is an easy way to see the future value of money, which we need to project what our expenses will be in the future and to get an estimate of what our investments will grow to. See the compounding table on page 226 to estimate both.

## For inflation

In the case of inflation, the future value of money will depend on the rate of inflation and how many years in the future you want to project.

For example, to see what Rs 1 lakh you spend today will be worth at 5 per cent inflation in ten years, you will need to use the tables to get the value.

Look at where 5 per cent rate and ten years meet – that value is 1.6289.

Multiply Rs 1 lakh with 1.6289 and the future value is Rs 1.63 lakh. We will round off to two decimals for the final number.

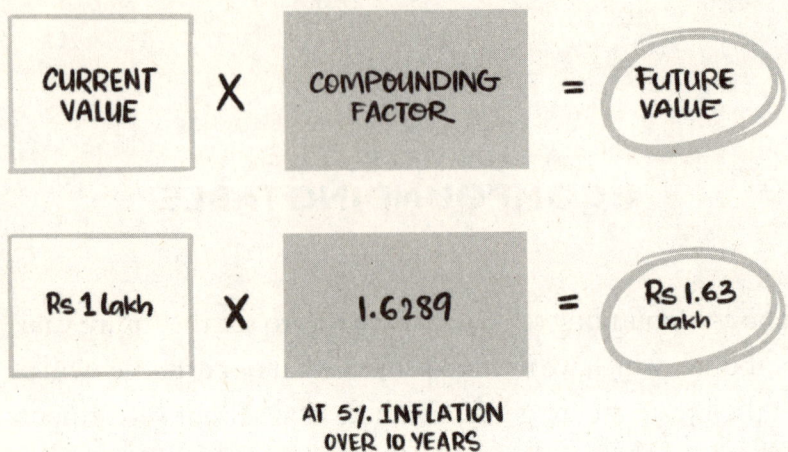

Likewise, to see the value of Rs 1 lakh at an inflation rate of 4 per cent in twenty years, look at where 4 per cent and twenty years meet—the value is 2.1911.

Multiply Rs 1 lakh with 2.1911 and the future value is Rs 2.19 lakh.

Use this as the base for forecasting how much you will need to spend in future years due to inflation. Use an inflation value of 5 per cent or 6 per cent, but if you think your personal expenses are inflating at a higher rate, feel free to raise the rate to do your calculations.

## For investments

This table can also be used to project the value of the investment into the future. If we know the number of years the investment will be at work and the expected rate of return, we can see what the money will grow to in the future.

# Worksheets

To see the future value of Rs 1 lakh at 12 per cent annual return for ten years, look where the 12 per cent and ten years meet in the table—the value is 3.1058.

Multiply Rs 1 lakh with 3.1058 and the future value is Rs 3.11 lakh.

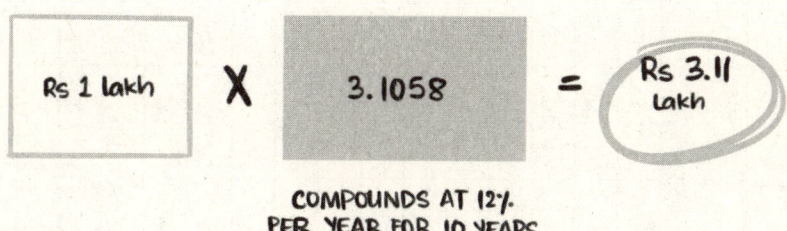

COMPOUNDS AT 12%
PER YEAR FOR 10 YEARS

See the future value of Rs 5 lakh that grows at 15 per cent for twenty years by looking at where 15 per cent and twenty years meet—the value is 16.3665.

Multiply Rs 5 lakh with 16.3665 and the future value is Rs 81.83 lakh.

You can use this to see how your money compounds over time as you invest at a given rate of return. It is a good idea to use a rate of return of 12 per cent for an index return on your equity investments and a rate of 5 per cent for your FD returns.

The more you engage with this table, the easier its use will be. The compounding table is a key tool in your money box to show you the future face of money.

## COMPOUNDING TABLE

| Rate / Year | 4% | 5% | 6% | 7% | 8% | 9% | 10% | 11% | 12% | 13% | 14% | 15% |
|---|---|---|---|---|---|---|---|---|---|---|---|---|
| 1 | 1.0400 | 1.0500 | 1.0600 | 1.0700 | 1.0800 | 1.0900 | 1.1000 | 1.1100 | 1.1200 | 1.1300 | 1.1400 | 1.1500 |
| 2 | 1.0816 | 1.1025 | 1.1236 | 1.1449 | 1.1664 | 1.1881 | 1.2100 | 1.2321 | 1.2544 | 1.2769 | 1.2996 | 1.3225 |
| 3 | 1.1249 | 1.1576 | 1.1910 | 1.2250 | 1.2597 | 1.2950 | 1.3310 | 1.3676 | 1.4049 | 1.4429 | 1.4815 | 1.5209 |
| 4 | 1.1699 | 1.2155 | 1.2625 | 1.3108 | 1.3605 | 1.4116 | 1.4641 | 1.5181 | 1.5735 | 1.6305 | 1.6890 | 1.7490 |
| 5 | 1.2167 | 1.2763 | 1.3382 | 1.4026 | 1.4693 | 1.5386 | 1.6105 | 1.6851 | 1.7623 | 1.8424 | 1.9254 | 2.0114 |
| 6 | 1.2653 | 1.3401 | 1.4185 | 1.5007 | 1.5869 | 1.6771 | 1.7716 | 1.8704 | 1.9738 | 2.0820 | 2.1950 | 2.3131 |
| 7 | 1.3159 | 1.4071 | 1.5036 | 1.6058 | 1.7138 | 1.8280 | 1.9487 | 2.0762 | 2.2107 | 2.3526 | 2.5023 | 2.6600 |
| 8 | 1.3686 | 1.4775 | 1.5938 | 1.7182 | 1.8509 | 1.9926 | 2.1436 | 2.3045 | 2.4760 | 2.6584 | 2.8526 | 3.0590 |
| 9 | 1.4233 | 1.5513 | 1.6895 | 1.8385 | 1.9990 | 2.1719 | 2.3579 | 2.5580 | 2.7731 | 3.0040 | 3.2519 | 3.5179 |
| 10 | 1.4802 | 1.6289 | 1.7908 | 1.9672 | 2.1589 | 2.3674 | 2.5937 | 2.8394 | 3.1058 | 3.3946 | 3.7072 | 4.0456 |
| 11 | 1.5395 | 1.7103 | 1.8983 | 2.1049 | 2.3316 | 2.5804 | 2.8531 | 3.1518 | 3.4785 | 3.8359 | 4.2262 | 4.6524 |
| 12 | 1.6010 | 1.7959 | 2.0122 | 2.2522 | 2.5182 | 2.8127 | 3.1384 | 3.4985 | 3.8960 | 4.3345 | 4.8179 | 5.3503 |
| 13 | 1.6651 | 1.8856 | 2.1329 | 2.4098 | 2.7196 | 3.0658 | 3.4523 | 3.8833 | 4.3635 | 4.8980 | 5.4924 | 6.1528 |
| 14 | 1.7317 | 1.9799 | 2.2609 | 2.5785 | 2.9372 | 3.3417 | 3.7975 | 4.3104 | 4.8871 | 5.5348 | 6.2613 | 7.0757 |
| 15 | 1.8009 | 2.0789 | 2.3966 | 2.7590 | 3.1722 | 3.6425 | 4.1772 | 4.7846 | 5.4736 | 6.2543 | 7.1379 | 8.1371 |

## Compounding Table

| Rate Year | 4% | 5% | 6% | 7% | 8% | 9% | 10% | 11% | 12% | 13% | 14% | 15% |
|---|---|---|---|---|---|---|---|---|---|---|---|---|
| 16 | 1.8730 | 2.1829 | 2.5404 | 2.9522 | 3.4259 | 3.9703 | 4.5950 | 5.3109 | 6.1304 | 7.0673 | 8.1372 | 9.3576 |
| 17 | 1.9479 | 2.2920 | 2.6928 | 3.1588 | 3.7000 | 4.3276 | 5.0545 | 5.8951 | 6.8660 | 7.9861 | 9.2765 | 10.7613 |
| 18 | 2.0258 | 2.4066 | 2.8543 | 3.3799 | 3.9960 | 4.7171 | 5.5599 | 6.5436 | 7.6900 | 9.0243 | 10.5752 | 12.3755 |
| 19 | 2.1068 | 2.5270 | 3.0256 | 3.6165 | 4.3157 | 5.1417 | 6.1159 | 7.2633 | 8.6128 | 10.1974 | 12.0557 | 14.2318 |
| 20 | 2.1911 | 2.6533 | 3.2071 | 3.8697 | 4.6610 | 5.6044 | 6.7275 | 8.0623 | 9.6463 | 11.5231 | 13.7435 | 16.3665 |
| 21 | 2.2788 | 2.7860 | 3.3996 | 4.1406 | 5.0338 | 6.1088 | 7.4002 | 8.9492 | 10.8038 | 13.0211 | 15.6676 | 18.8215 |
| 22 | 2.3699 | 2.9253 | 3.6035 | 4.4304 | 5.4365 | 6.6586 | 8.1403 | 9.9336 | 12.1003 | 14.7138 | 17.8610 | 21.6447 |
| 23 | 2.4647 | 3.0715 | 3.8197 | 4.7405 | 5.8715 | 7.2579 | 8.9543 | 11.0263 | 13.5523 | 16.6266 | 20.3616 | 24.8915 |
| 24 | 2.5633 | 3.2251 | 4.0489 | 5.0724 | 6.3412 | 7.9111 | 9.8497 | 12.2392 | 15.1786 | 18.7881 | 23.2122 | 28.6252 |
| 25 | 2.6658 | 3.3864 | 4.2919 | 5.4274 | 6.8485 | 8.6231 | 10.8347 | 13.5855 | 17.0001 | 21.2305 | 26.4619 | 32.9190 |
| 26 | 2.7725 | 3.5557 | 4.5494 | 5.8074 | 7.3964 | 9.3992 | 11.9182 | 15.0799 | 19.0401 | 23.9905 | 30.1666 | 37.8568 |
| 27 | 2.8834 | 3.7335 | 4.8223 | 6.2139 | 7.9881 | 10.2451 | 13.1100 | 16.7386 | 21.3249 | 27.1093 | 34.3899 | 43.5353 |
| 28 | 2.9987 | 3.9201 | 5.1117 | 6.6488 | 8.6271 | 11.1671 | 14.4210 | 18.5799 | 23.8839 | 30.6335 | 39.2045 | 50.0656 |
| 29 | 3.1187 | 4.1161 | 5.4184 | 7.1143 | 9.3173 | 12.1722 | 15.8631 | 20.6237 | 26.7499 | 34.6158 | 44.6931 | 57.5755 |
| 30 | 3.2434 | 4.3219 | 5.7435 | 7.6123 | 10.0627 | 13.2677 | 17.4494 | 22.8923 | 29.9599 | 39.1159 | 50.9502 | 66.2118 |

# 5: ANNUAL SAVINGS TABLE

The annual savings table is a way to understand how much you need to save each year to hit a future target of money. You need to know the value of the goal you target, the number of years to the goal and the rate of return that you expect.

## Sample annual savings

If you want to target Rs 25 lakh in four years, with your savings growing at 7 per cent, then this is how you need to use the table on page 230 by looking where 7 per cent and four years meet—the value is 0.2252.

Multiply Rs 25 lakh by 0.2252 and the future value is Rs 5,63,070.

You need to save Rs 5.63 lakh a year or Rs 47,000 a month.

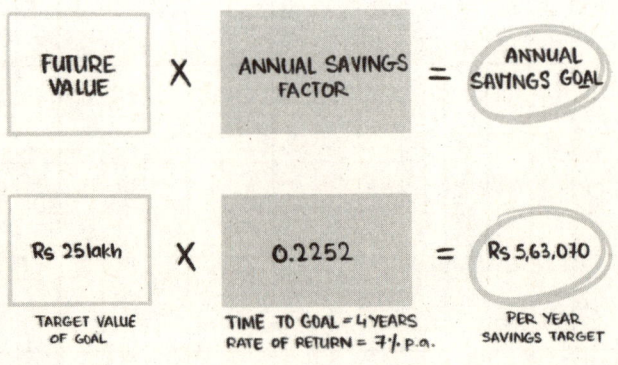

## Your annual savings

If you want to target Rs 500 lakh, that is, Rs 5 crore, in twenty years and anticipate that you can earn 12 per cent a year return, then see where 12 per cent and twenty years meet—the value is 0.0139.

Multiply Rs 500 lakh by 0.0139 and the future value is Rs 6,93,939.

You need to save Rs 6.94 lakh a year or approximately Rs 58,000 a month.

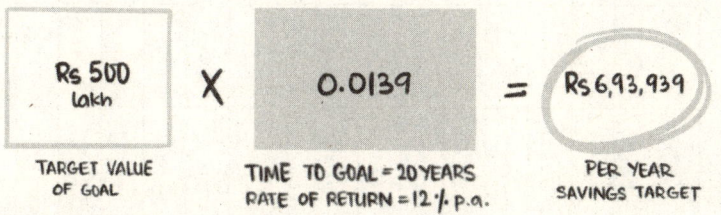

Therefore, you can use the annual savings table to work backwards to see the current saving needs for future goals.

You can also use this table for multiple goals and adjust the value of the goals to see what the impact of raising or lowering the goal might be on current savings needs.

For short-term goals of up to three years, it is a good idea to use a growth rate of 5 per cent.

For medium-term goals of up to seven years, it is a good idea to use a growth rate of 7–8 per cent.

For long-term goals of ten years or more, it is a good idea to use a growth rate of 12–14 per cent.

## WORKSHEETS

### ANNUAL SAVINGS TABLE

| Rate\Year | 4% | 5% | 6% | 7% | 8% | 9% | 10% | 11% | 12% | 13% | 14% | 15% |
|---|---|---|---|---|---|---|---|---|---|---|---|---|
| 1 | 1.0000 | 1.0000 | 1.0000 | 1.0000 | 1.0000 | 1.0000 | 1.0000 | 1.0000 | 1.0000 | 1.0000 | 1.0000 | 1.0000 |
| 2 | 0.4902 | 0.4878 | 0.4854 | 0.4831 | 0.4808 | 0.4785 | 0.4762 | 0.4739 | 0.4717 | 0.4695 | 0.4673 | 0.4651 |
| 3 | 0.3203 | 0.3172 | 0.3141 | 0.3111 | 0.3080 | 0.3051 | 0.3021 | 0.2992 | 0.2963 | 0.2935 | 0.2907 | 0.2880 |
| 4 | 0.2355 | 0.2320 | 0.2286 | 0.2252 | 0.2219 | 0.2187 | 0.2155 | 0.2123 | 0.2092 | 0.2062 | 0.2032 | 0.2003 |
| 5 | 0.1846 | 0.1810 | 0.1774 | 0.1739 | 0.1705 | 0.1671 | 0.1638 | 0.1606 | 0.1574 | 0.1543 | 0.1513 | 0.1483 |
| 6 | 0.1508 | 0.1470 | 0.1434 | 0.1398 | 0.1363 | 0.1329 | 0.1296 | 0.1264 | 0.1232 | 0.1202 | 0.1172 | 0.1142 |
| 7 | 0.1266 | 0.1228 | 0.1191 | 0.1156 | 0.1121 | 0.1087 | 0.1054 | 0.1022 | 0.0991 | 0.0961 | 0.0932 | 0.0904 |
| 8 | 0.1085 | 0.1047 | 0.1010 | 0.0975 | 0.0940 | 0.0907 | 0.0874 | 0.0843 | 0.0813 | 0.0784 | 0.0756 | 0.0729 |
| 9 | 0.0945 | 0.0907 | 0.0870 | 0.0835 | 0.0801 | 0.0768 | 0.0736 | 0.0706 | 0.0677 | 0.0649 | 0.0622 | 0.0596 |
| 10 | 0.0833 | 0.0795 | 0.0759 | 0.0724 | 0.0690 | 0.0658 | 0.0627 | 0.0598 | 0.0570 | 0.0543 | 0.0517 | 0.0493 |
| 11 | 0.0741 | 0.0704 | 0.0668 | 0.0634 | 0.0601 | 0.0569 | 0.0540 | 0.0511 | 0.0484 | 0.0458 | 0.0434 | 0.0411 |
| 12 | 0.0666 | 0.0628 | 0.0593 | 0.0559 | 0.0527 | 0.0497 | 0.0468 | 0.0440 | 0.0414 | 0.0390 | 0.0367 | 0.0345 |
| 13 | 0.0601 | 0.0565 | 0.0530 | 0.0497 | 0.0465 | 0.0436 | 0.0408 | 0.0382 | 0.0357 | 0.0334 | 0.0312 | 0.0291 |
| 14 | 0.0547 | 0.0510 | 0.0476 | 0.0443 | 0.0413 | 0.0384 | 0.0357 | 0.0332 | 0.0309 | 0.0287 | 0.0266 | 0.0247 |
| 15 | 0.0499 | 0.0463 | 0.0430 | 0.0398 | 0.0368 | 0.0341 | 0.0315 | 0.0291 | 0.0268 | 0.0247 | 0.0228 | 0.0210 |

## ANNUAL SAVINGS TABLE

| Rate Year | 4% | 5% | 6% | 7% | 8% | 9% | 10% | 11% | 12% | 13% | 14% | 15% |
|---|---|---|---|---|---|---|---|---|---|---|---|---|
| 16 | 0.0458 | 0.0423 | 0.0390 | 0.0359 | 0.0330 | 0.0303 | 0.0278 | 0.0255 | 0.0234 | 0.0214 | 0.0196 | 0.0179 |
| 17 | 0.0422 | 0.0387 | 0.0354 | 0.0324 | 0.0296 | 0.0270 | 0.0247 | 0.0225 | 0.0205 | 0.0186 | 0.0169 | 0.0154 |
| 18 | 0.0390 | 0.0355 | 0.0324 | 0.0294 | 0.0267 | 0.0242 | 0.0219 | 0.0198 | 0.0179 | 0.0162 | 0.0146 | 0.0132 |
| 19 | 0.0361 | 0.0327 | 0.0296 | 0.0268 | 0.0241 | 0.0217 | 0.0195 | 0.0176 | 0.0158 | 0.0141 | 0.0127 | 0.0113 |
| 20 | 0.0336 | 0.0302 | 0.0272 | 0.0244 | 0.0219 | 0.0195 | 0.0175 | 0.0156 | 0.0139 | 0.0124 | 0.0110 | 0.0098 |
| 21 | 0.0313 | 0.0280 | 0.0250 | 0.0223 | 0.0198 | 0.0176 | 0.0156 | 0.0138 | 0.0122 | 0.0108 | 0.0095 | 0.0084 |
| 22 | 0.0292 | 0.0260 | 0.0230 | 0.0204 | 0.0180 | 0.0159 | 0.0140 | 0.0123 | 0.0108 | 0.0095 | 0.0083 | 0.0073 |
| 23 | 0.0273 | 0.0241 | 0.0213 | 0.0187 | 0.0164 | 0.0144 | 0.0126 | 0.0110 | 0.0096 | 0.0083 | 0.0072 | 0.0063 |
| 24 | 0.0256 | 0.0225 | 0.0197 | 0.0172 | 0.0150 | 0.0130 | 0.0113 | 0.0098 | 0.0085 | 0.0073 | 0.0063 | 0.0054 |
| 25 | 0.0240 | 0.0210 | 0.0182 | 0.0158 | 0.0137 | 0.0118 | 0.0102 | 0.0087 | 0.0075 | 0.0064 | 0.0055 | 0.0047 |
| 26 | 0.0226 | 0.0196 | 0.0169 | 0.0146 | 0.0125 | 0.0107 | 0.0092 | 0.0078 | 0.0067 | 0.0057 | 0.0048 | 0.0041 |
| 27 | 0.0212 | 0.0183 | 0.0157 | 0.0134 | 0.0114 | 0.0097 | 0.0083 | 0.0070 | 0.0059 | 0.0050 | 0.0042 | 0.0035 |
| 28 | 0.0200 | 0.0171 | 0.0146 | 0.0124 | 0.0105 | 0.0089 | 0.0075 | 0.0063 | 0.0052 | 0.0044 | 0.0037 | 0.0031 |
| 29 | 0.0189 | 0.0160 | 0.0136 | 0.0114 | 0.0096 | 0.0081 | 0.0067 | 0.0056 | 0.0047 | 0.0039 | 0.0032 | 0.0027 |
| 30 | 0.0178 | 0.0151 | 0.0126 | 0.0106 | 0.0088 | 0.0073 | 0.0061 | 0.0050 | 0.0041 | 0.0034 | 0.0028 | 0.0023 |

# 6: ALMOST-THERE GOALS WORKSHEET

Goals that are within three years are called Almost-There goals. There is a two-step method to calculate how much you need to save for these goals.

First, define your goal. In the sample taken, the goal of down payment for a home is three years away. The current value of the down payment is Rs 40 lakh. The inflation assumption is 5 per cent.

Step 1. Estimate what the goal will cost three years later at the chosen rate of inflation.

Use the compounding table given earlier to inflate the number of Rs 40 lakh. The number where three years and 5 per cent meet is the value 1.1576.

Multiply Rs 40 lakh with 1.1576 to get a future value of Rs 46.31 lakh.

1. Estimate Future Value

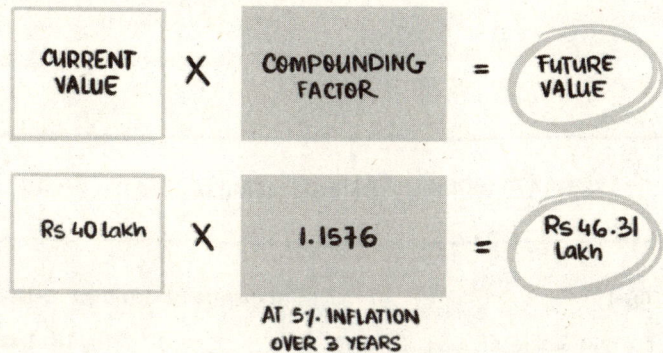

Step 2. Now, to estimate the annual savings needed.

The estimated return is taken as 6 per cent. The number where three years and 6 per cent meet in the annual savings table is 0.3141.

Multiply Rs 46.31 lakh by 0.3141 to get the annual savings needed of Rs 14.55 lakh, or approximately Rs 1.21 lakh a month.

2. Estimate Annual Savings Needed

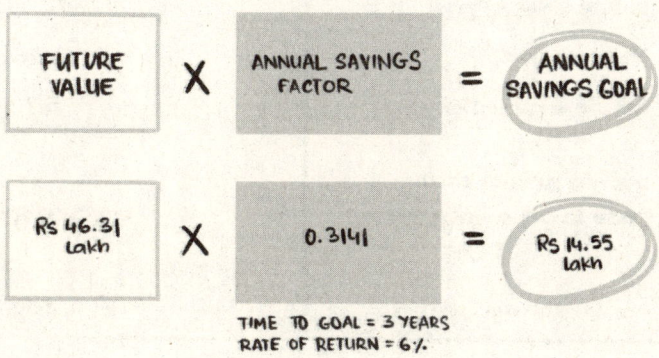

Now use the same method to write down your own goals.

*Note*: Final numbers have been rounded off to two decimal points.

Choose an inflation rate of 5 per cent and a return rate of 5-6 per cent to be on the conservative side for a goal that is within three years away.

| SAMPLE WORKSHEET FOR ALMOST-THERE GOALS ||
|---|---|
| Goal | Downpayment of house |
| Current value of goal | Rs 40 lakh |
| Years to goal | 3 years |
| Inflation rate | 5% |
| **STEP 1** | |
| Use compounding table to get future value of goal | 40 X 1.1576 |
| Target amount | Rs 46.31 lakh |
| **STEP 2** | |
| Future value of goal | Rs 46.31 lakh |
| Years to goal | 3 years |
| Return expectation | 6% |
| Use the annual saving table to get savings needed | 46.31 X 0.3141 |
| Annual savings needed | Rs 14.55 lakh |

## YOUR WORKSHEET FOR ALMOST-THERE GOALS

| | |
|---|---|
| **Goal** | |
| Current value of goal | |
| Years to goal | |
| Inflation rate | |
| **STEP 1** Use compounding table to get future value of goal | |
| Target amount | |
| **STEP 2** | |
| Future value of goal | |
| Years to goal | |
| Return expectation | |
| Use the annual savings table to get savings needed | |
| Annual savings needed | |

# 7: IN-SOME-TIME GOALS WORKSHEET

Goals that are between three and seven years are called In-Some-Time goals. There is a two-step method to calculate how much you need to save for these goals.

First, define the goal. In the sample, we have used the goal of a child's education that is seven years away. The current value of the education is Rs 100 lakh, or Rs 1 crore. The inflation assumption is 5 per cent.

Step 1. Estimate what the goal will cost seven years later at the chosen rate of inflation.

Use the compounding table to inflate the number of Rs 100 lakh. The number where seven years and 5 per cent meet is the value 1.4071.

Multiply Rs 100 lakh by 1.4071 to see a future value of Rs 140.71 lakh.

1. Estimate Future Value

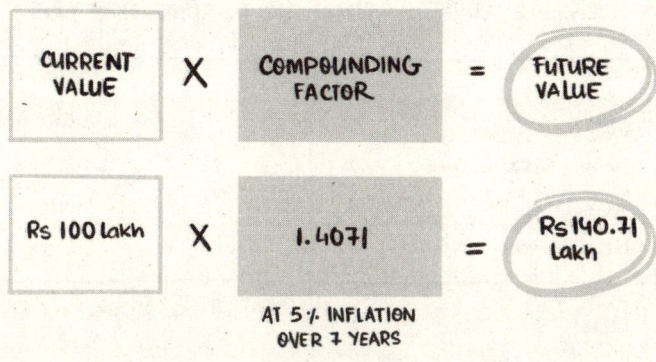

Step 2. Now, to estimate the annual savings needed.

The estimated return is taken as 10 per cent. The number where seven years and 10 per cent meet in the annual savings table is 0.1054.

Multiply Rs 140.71 lakh by 0.1054 to get the annual saving needed of Rs 14.83 lakh, or approximately Rs 1.24 lakh a month.

2. Estimate Annual Savings Needed

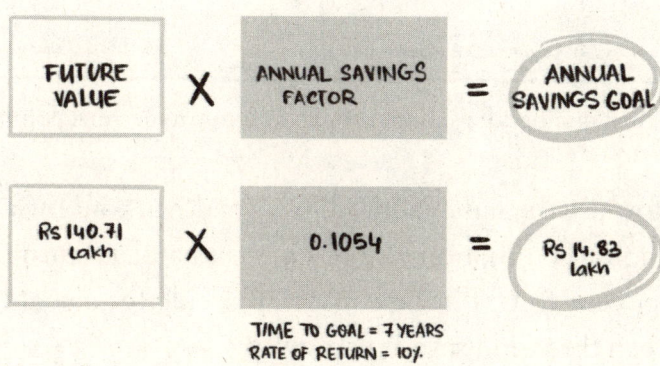

| SAMPLE WORKSHEET FOR AN IN-SOME-TIME GOAL ||
| --- | --- |
| Goal | Child's education |
| Current value of goal | Rs 100 lakh |
| Years to goal | 7 years |
| Inflation rate | 5% |
| **STEP 1** <br> Use compounding table to get future value of goal | 100 × 1.4071 |
| Target amount | Rs 140.71 lakh |
| **STEP 2** | |
| Future value of goal | Rs 140.71 lakh |
| Years to goal | 7 years |
| Return expectation | 10% |
| Use the annual savings table to get savings needed | 140.71 × 0.1054 |
| Annual savings needed | Rs 14.83 lakh |

*Note*: Final numbers have been rounded off to two decimal points.

Now use the same method to write down your own goals.

Choose an inflation rate of 5 per cent and a return rate of 10 per cent to be on the conservative side for a goal that is between three and seven years away.

| YOUR WORKSHEET FOR AN IN-SOME-TIME GOAL | |
|---|---|
| Goal | |
| Current value of goal | |
| Years to goal | |
| Inflation rate | |
| **STEP 1** Use compounding table to get future value of goal | |
| Target amount | |
| **STEP 2** | |
| Future value of goal | |
| Years to goal | |
| Return expectation | |
| Use the annual savings table to get savings needed | |
| Annual savings needed | |

# 8: FAR-AWAY GOALS WORKSHEET

Goals that are beyond seven years are called Far-Away goals. There is a two-step method to calculate how much you need to save for these goals.

First, define your goal. In the sample, we have used the goal of a child's marriage that is fifteen years away. The current value of the wedding is Rs 50 lakh. The inflation assumption is 5 per cent.

**Step 1.** Estimate what the goal will cost fifteen years later at the chosen rate of inflation.

Use the compounding table to inflate the number of Rs 50 lakh. The number where fifteen years and 5 per cent meet is the value 2.0789.

Multiply Rs 50 lakh with 2.0789 to see a future value of Rs 103.95 lakh, that is, Rs 1.04 crore.

## 1. Estimate Future Value

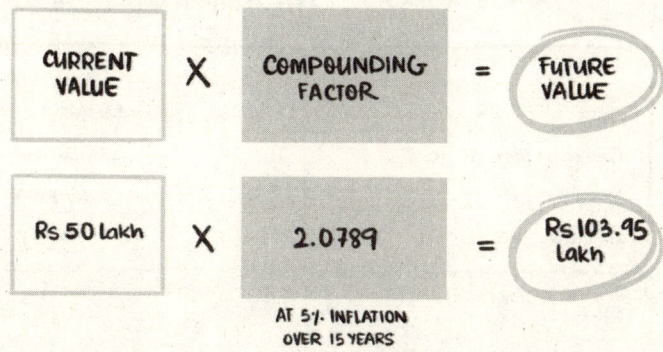

Step 2. Now to estimate the annual savings needed.

The estimated return is taken as 12 per cent. The number where fifteen years and 12 per cent meet in the annual savings table is 0.0268.

Multiply Rs 103.95 lakh by 0.0268 to get the annual savings needed of Rs 2.79 lakh, or approximately Rs 23,237 a month.

## 2. Estimate Annual Savings Needed

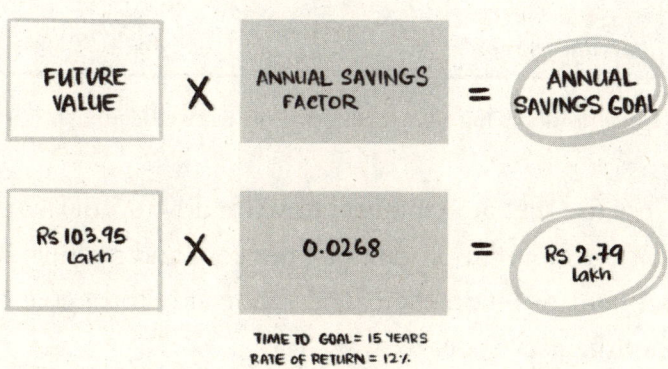

| SAMPLE WORKSHEET FOR A FAR-AWAY GOAL ||
|---|---|
| Goal | Child's marriage |
| Current value of goal | Rs 50 lakh |
| Years to goal | 15 years |
| Inflation rate | 5% |
| **STEP 1** | |
| Use compounding table to get future value of goal | 50 X 2.0789 |
| Target amount | Rs 103.95 lakh |
| **STEP 2** | |
| Future value of goal | Rs 103.95 lakh |
| Years to goal | 15 years |
| Return expectation | 12% |
| Use the annual savings table to get savings needed | 103.95 X .0268 |
| Annual savings needed | Rs 2.79 lakh |

*Note:* Final numbers have been rounded off to two decimal points.

Now use the same method to write down your own goals. Choose an inflation rate of 5 per cent and a return rate of 12 per cent to be on the conservative side for a goal that is further than seven years away.

## YOUR WORKSHEET FOR A FAR-AWAY GOAL

**Goal**
Current value of goal
Years to goal
Inflation rate

**STEP 1**
Use compounding table to get future value of goal

Target amount

**STEP 2**
Future value of goal
Years to goal
Return expectation

Use the annual savings table to get savings needed

Annual savings needed

## 9: RETIREMENT WORKSHEET

This is a three-step method to calculate how much is enough for retirement and how to get there.

Step 1. Estimate the annual expenditure at age sixty. We already have a number for your annual expenditure from the cash-flow statement. In the sample sheet, we have used Rs 12 lakh as annual expenditure. We have also assumed that retirement is twenty-five years later. Inflation rate has been assumed at 5 per cent to calculate the annual expense at age sixty. This will be Rs 12 lakh multiplied by the value in the compounding table where twenty-five years and 5 per cent meet—the value is 3.3864.

Multiply Rs 12 lakh by 3.3864 to get a future annual expense at age sixty of Rs 40.64 lakh.

1. Estimate Future Value

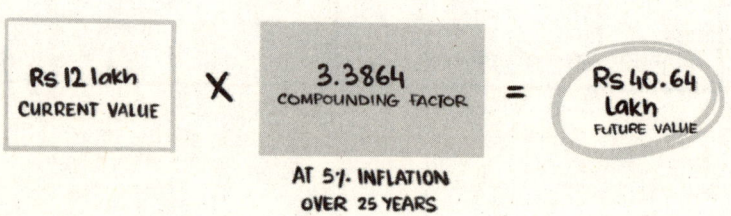

Step 2. Estimate what the corpus requirement will be for this annual expenditure that will grow at a 5 per cent a year rate due to inflation. A rule of thumb multiplier of twenty-six is used to see the value of the target corpus. Read chapter 11 on retirement to understand where the twenty-six multiplier came from.

Multiply Rs 40.64 lakh by twenty-six to get a corpus value of Rs 1056.54 lakh, that is, Rs 10.57 crore.

2. Estimate Retirement Corpus

Step 3. Estimate how much you need to save a year to reach the target of Rs 10.57 crore.

The goal is twenty-five years away.

The rate of return is assumed to be 14 per cent.

Use the annual savings table to see the value where twenty-five years and 14 per cent meet to get the value 0.0055.

Multiply Rs 1056.54 lakh by 0.0055 to get an annual saving target of Rs 5.81 lakh, that is, approximately Rs 48,411 a month.

## 3. Estimate Annual Savings Needed

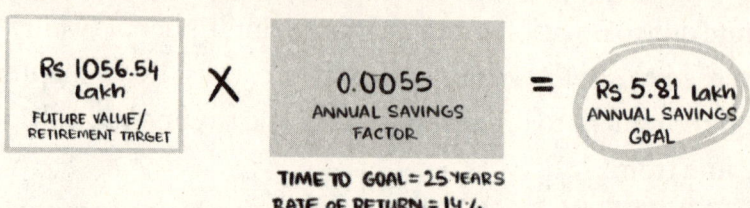

Now use the same method to write down your own goals. Choose an inflation rate of 5 per cent and a return rate of 14 per cent to be on the conservative side for a goal that is beyond ten years in the future.

# SAMPLE WORKSHEET FOR RETIREMENT

| | |
|---|---|
| Goal | Retirement |
| Years to goal | 25 Years |
| Current annual expense | 12 lakh |
| Inflation rate | 5% |
| **STEP 1** Use compounding table to get future value of goal | 12 × 3.3864 |
| Annual expenditure at age 60 | Rs 40.64 lakh |
| **STEP 2** Future value of goal × 26 (use a multiplier of 26 to forecast retirement corpus) | Rs 40.64 lakh × 26 |
| Retirement corpus needed | Rs 1056.54 lakh |
| **STEP 3** | |
| Goal target | Rs 1,056.54 lakh |
| Return expectation | 14% |
| Years to goal | 25 |
| Use the annual savings table to get savings needed | 1,056.54 × 0.0055 = |
| Annual savings needed | Rs 5.81 lakh |

*Note*: Final numbers have been rounded off to two decimal points.

# YOUR WORKSHEET FOR RETIREMENT

| | |
|---|---|
| Goal | |
| Years to goal | |
| Current annual expense | |
| Inflation rate | |
| **STEP 1** | |
| Use compounding table to get future value of goal | |
| Annual expenditure at age 60 | |
| **STEP 2** | |
| Future Value of goal X 26 (use a multiplier of 26 to forecast retirement corpus) | |
| Retirement corpus needed | |
| **STEP 3** | |
| Goal target | |
| Return expectation | |
| Years to goal | |
| Use the annual savings table to get savings needed | |
| Annual savings needed | |

# APPENDIX

*Calculations and assumptions for post-retirement expenditure and savings.*

We need to make several forecasts. I'll list them out, and if you feel something is too large or too small, you can tweak the final rule of thumb accordingly.

Assumption one: Your income will grow every year at 10 per cent. This is a reasonable assumption, because even if you don't get a 10 per cent increment each year, the salary jump whenever you change a job compensates for two years of flat raises.

Assumption two: Your current expenditure and inflation grow at 6 per cent. I've overstated inflation here because of our past experience with inflation. Irresponsible governments cause inflation and we don't know what our vibrant democracy will throw into the parliament next. The current government is prudent and, in 2024, is committed to an inflation target of 4 per cent with a plus-or-minus band of 2 per cent, which means that the central bank will target inflation between 2 per cent and 6 per cent, but will aim to keep it near 4 per cent. But this can change very quickly with a less responsible government; therefore, I'm taking a 6 per cent number.

Assumption three: Your investments grow at a conservative 10 per cent a year while you are working. In a 6 per cent inflation regime, the risk-free return, or return from products like the PPF or EPF, is usually 1 or 2 percentage points higher than inflation.

It is reasonable to assume a risk-free return of 8 per cent. But you have some equity-linked products in your portfolio that will grow over the long term at about 12 per cent. Again, equity return is linked to the overall GDP growth of a country plus inflation, plus an equity risk premium.

An equity risk premium is the extra return over the risk-free return that equity earns to compensate for the risk. So if an economy is growing at 8 per cent a year, with 6 per cent inflation, we can assume an equity return of 15–16 per cent a year. But I will stay conservative and assume just a 12 per cent equity return, and then take an average return of 10 per cent overall return.

After you read this book and understand how equity investing works, I'm hoping that you can target a return that is much higher than 10 per cent. If you do that, your savings ratio goes down. But let's stay conservative. Notice that in this system, you don't consume all of your annual salary hike. Salary grows at 10 per cent but expenses grow at 6 per cent. This difference between your salary hike and spending is what you will save for the rest of your goals.

Too theoretical? So, let's say you are thirty years old, and earn Rs 6 lakhs post tax a year. You save 30 per cent of this income and eat up Rs 4.2 lakhs a year. You invest your savings of Rs 1.8 lakhs in a mix of products – PF, PPF and a couple of equity funds. You target a 'safe' return of 10 per cent a year on this saving.

Now at age thirty-one, you get your increment at work and your post-tax income grows by 10 per cent. You now get Rs 6.6 lakhs a year. You don't consume all of the increment, but your spending grows in line with inflation, which we take at 6 per cent. Your second-year saving is Rs 1.98 lakhs. This gets added to the total of your last year's saving and the return on that.

We keep doing this exercise till you hit age sixty. Do you know how much money you'd have got? Rs 10.7 crores. Yup. That's the power of compounding, regular saving and a reasonable return. Now you look like your dad or mum looks today. Creepy, no? *Anyhoo*. Onwards to old age.

Assumption one: You will spend 70 per cent of your pre-retirement expenditure at age sixty. Remember that the spending is rising at 6 per cent; so if you spent Rs 4.2 lakhs a year at age thirty, by age sixty you are spending an annual amount of Rs 24 lakhs. There is a bunch of costs that go towards maintaining our work-related lives –

travel, clothes, lunch, coffee, work-related socializing and so on. These costs go down once you retire; therefore, we take 70 per cent of your spending at age sixty as the amount you will spend at age sixty-one, or you will spend just under Rs 17 lakhs a year at age sixty-one. If you think you will continue to spend an equal amount, bump up the rule of thumb a notch and look at a higher saving ratio or target a higher return ratio.

Assumption two: Your post-retirement expenses continue to grow at 6 per cent a year. So, by age sixty-five, you will be spending an annual Rs 21 lakhs and so on.

Assumption three: You will leave your entire corpus to your kids and will not use a single rupee of your retirement corpus. If you plan to use your capital during retirement, your saving ratio will go down.

Assumption four: You split your retirement corpus at sixty into two parts. Seventy per cent of the corpus goes into a conservative 7 per cent guaranteed-return product, like an FD or a debt fund. Again, this 7 per cent number is relative to the 6 per cent inflation number. If you want to work with a lower inflation number, take 1 percentage point above that as your guaranteed return for post-retirement income. Rs 70 out of every Rs 100 you are putting to work for assured income starting at age sixty. Rs 30 of every Rs 100, or 30 per cent of your corpus, you can invest in lower-risk equity funds — maybe a low-cost index fund. We don't need this money for the next twenty years. I assume a conservative 10 per cent return on the equity portfolio.

The income you draw is much larger than your annual expense at age sixty. You do this because inflation will make you need progressively more money each year; and instead of rejigging your portfolio every other year, we leave that for just once in the future.

There can be a more efficient way to do this, but remember, this is an indicative method. A real financial plan will be much more dynamic than just a one reset of your portfolio. Your income is much larger than your expenses and will continue to be till you hit age eighty. For twenty years, 70 per cent of your portfolio will generate enough inflation-adjusted income. What'll you do with the annual or monthly savings? Invest it right back – into the same fund that 30 per cent of your corpus went into. The monthly savings go into an SIP and get to work in the same fund. So you have a growing corpus for your really old age. At age eighty, inflation will catch up with your income. That's the time you liquidate your portfolio and put everything in the safe 7 per cent product. There is enough money to last you till you are 111. Not only is your corpus still there, it has also grown over time. This is almost the worst case. You can do much better than this. And the saving ratio you need can be much lower.

You are sixty. Your kids are now your age today. And you find yourself telling them stuff that your dad says today that irritates the hell out of you. Circle of life, my friend. Note to my future self: *Never* say 'When I was your age ...' So you are now a rich old man with over Rs 10 crores under your belt.

Yeah, your clothes have shrunk specially over the middle and you need better glasses, for you can't see your toes any more when standing straight. At retirement at sixty, you'll need 70 per cent of the expenditure of your working self, or Rs 16.88 lakhs a year or Rs 1.4 lakhs a month.

Remember, your retirement kitty was just over Rs 10 crores; you are drawing income from Rs 7 crores and have put away Rs 3 crores in equity mutual funds for the future. At 7 per cent, the investment of Rs 7 crores gives you an annual income of just over Rs 52 lakhs, but you need only about Rs 17 lakhs. You invest back the extra into the equity mutual fund product. Now, your expense at age sixty-one will grow at 6 per cent a year, and each year you need more and more income just to retain your purchasing power.

So by age sixty-five, you will need about Rs 21 lakhs a year or almost Rs 2 lakhs a month. By age seventy-five, you need just over Rs 3 lakhs a month. By age ninety, you need almost Rs 8 lakhs a month. If these numbers sound bizarre, just listen in to the really old people chatting in the park or at family dos, and you will hear the complaint against inflation. As a kid, I remember getting irritated whenever the old people would get together. Now they'll start talking about how expensive everything is, I used to mutter. Back in those days, kids couldn't utter aloud all the insidious little comments that were swimming around in their heads when adults were around. 'Arrey, on a salary of Rs 20 you could run the house and then have something left over? That shawl

Mamijee wears, no? That cost a full Rs 5. Now you can't buy it for five thousand only.'

Everybody shakes their heads. 'Tch tch. *Zamana hi kharab hai*' (these are bad times). As a kid, I remember buying sweets for five paise and bus tickets cost twenty-five paise (and I'm on my way to irritating the life out of kids in the family). My daughter has never seen coins below Re 1. Her daughter will probably say the same for fifty bucks. The fall in purchasing power is the reason that we worry about meeting our expenses when we retire. This calculation is meant to give a basic understanding of the many variables involved in doing the retirement calculation. It is, at best, indicative. You must use an online calculator or work with a planner for your unique retirement strategy.

# LAST NOTE

A few years back, I was sitting at café Le Morgan in Auroville with some Aurovillian friends and my family, soaking in the atmosphere and the coffee. It was very peaceful, made even more calm post a visit to the Matrimandir. Suddenly a man walked up and said: 'Monika Halan herself!'

We all looked up a bit shocked at this abrupt comment. Six heads turned to look at him. He then spoke further. 'You are the reason I am here.' It seems that he had called on my NDTV show, asking if he could retire early. He'd sent his portfolio and his pension amounts.

A bell rang in my head and I said, 'You're the army guy!' I remembered telling an army officer who wanted to take early retirement that his money was enough to go free. And here he was. In Auroville, living his dream life.

Each time I meet a reader or caller from my TV shows, or someone writes in to tell me that my writing or advice made a difference to their lives, I hit a personal high. I think I levitate a bit that day! One of the most common comments I get is around preventing people from making bad decisions. 'You are the reason I don't have ULIPs in my portfolio.' Or 'Because of you, I got saved from the insurance scam', or 'Your writing has made me a better investor'.

I have not met a single person who has said: 'You have made me rich overnight.' The goal is empowerment and financial freedom and not being suddenly super rich. Financial freedom and a feeling of being in control can happen even when you are not super rich.

Those who peddle dreams of making you rich, giving you the secret to becoming wealthy overnight, are pressing very old buttons. These buttons are greed and exclusivity. The greed button, when pressed, triggers the desire to get something by not doing much. It is the desire for disproportional gain.

Invest in this, you will double your money in one year. Or catch that upcoming real-estate deal and you will triple your money. Seriously, if the guy had a system that got him rich, why's he peddling books that will make him rich when people buy it to get his secret?

Exclusivity is the other button. We all believe that we are special, and we are. But at a fundamental level, this button gets pressed when you begin to believe that you know something that nobody else knows and, therefore, will make money.

The deal is now and not many people know about it; get in fast or you will lose the opportunity. This is a snake oil sales spiel that works so well to get people to make hasty punts with their money. Ask yourself this question – why is this person choosing you to be the one to get this super deal? If it was so good, why is he not borrowing money and putting more himself? Has he run out of relatives and friends that he is coming to you? He is pressing the 'you are the best; therefore, I am coming to you' button in you.

The book you just finished does not promise to make you rich overnight, or give you a road that only you can follow. There is nothing exclusive in this book. What you now have is an approach to money management, a system that sets you free from your everyday worries about money.

It empowers you to take decisions about your money today that will have a deep bearing on you tomorrow. It helps you build financial security using financial products. It helps you target your goals. If you have understood the message in the book, you will know that chasing a high return is not a smart thing to do. Chasing a financial goal, using an appropriate product is the smart way.

There is no secret mantra of money management in this book that will evaporate if too many people hear about it. The approach the book recommends is an open road – the more people who use the road, the better it gets. Sheer demand will put pressure on the financial sector to manufacture and sell financial products that are fair and transparent. The financial planning process is a path through dangerous waters, and you must share it with all your friends and family to stop them falling into the tricks and traps laid out by big finance.

Lastly, each piece of advice I write in the book is something that I have myself used. Emergency funds to medical cover to having my go-free money in place ten years ahead of my official retirement age! The system may be boring, but it works.

I have grown and been enriched by your mails and calls, and from personal meetings with you on the road, on airports, at conferences and in cafes. I'd love to continue the conversation and make the book better by the time we do the next print. Do ask your questions and suggest more areas that you need help in, and I will keep the conversation going. You can reach me on twitter at @monikahalan or on my site www.monikahalan.com

# ACKNOWLEDGEMENTS

To my gurus, The Mother and Sri Aurobindo, for finding me!

To the wonderful team at HarperCollins India. I'm delighted to work with professionals like you. Special shout-out to Ananth Padmanabhan and Sachin Sharma for their continued support with not just the mother book but all the translations and new editions.

*Let's Talk Money* is now present in Hindi, Marathi, Punjabi and Malayalam, and more languages are on the cards.

To the editor of the third edition, Shreya Lall at HarperCollins, for the minute work of introducing changes in the book. A thank you to the audiobook people at HarperCollins, and especially to Arcopol Chaudhuri, who heads the new media team, for all the digital and audio extensions that the book has seen over the years.

To Bonita Shimray – I will never forget the saree-picking sorties as we hunted for the perfect one for the cover in 2018. To Kavita C. Dikshit for catching that moment that was Let's Talk Money in her bestseller-selling picture on the cover. The shoot with my (now late) Toofan dog flopping in on all the frames and muscling into the team lunch later was something I will always remember and cherish.

To Rukmini Chawla for being the first person ever to identify the book in me way back in 2014. To Manisha Natarajan, my friend and TV partner – our money talks are still remembered by so many viewers. To Vivek Law, a partner in the financial-literacy journey and a perfect TV buddy as we did the Smart Money show together for years.

To my wonderful readers, viewers and listeners of my books, columns, videos, lectures, workshops and podcasts. Your enthusiasm, feedback and love keeps my work enriched. Years after the first edition came to the market, you still reach out to me every day with either a comment or a question, or sometimes just to tell me your money stories. Each mail and message is precious to me and I try and answer as many as I can. Keep them coming!

For the third edition, a special thank you to my kind readers who suggested corrections and helped me make this book better. Mahi S. Nair – thank you. Also to Jyotiprakash Raman, retired DGM, State Bank of India, who has painstakingly suggested minute changes to the text and has carried out a very detailed audit of the book. I have taken your suggestions and incorporated most of them. Thank you for this effort.

Gratitude to graphic artist Tanvi Agarwal (Sillystrokes) who has used her creativity to turn dense concepts into approachable illustrations and worksheets. Extremely talented, she is the artist who has internalized the book to work on these insightful illustrations. I must tell you how we got together: Somebody introduced her to me on Twitter. I replied, found her to be very enthusiastic, introduced her to HarperCollins, and that was the beginning of this wonderful association.

To my parents, (late) Mridula and Yogesh Halan, for always being there. Your past has made my future possible. To my husband, Gautam Chikermane, for making the pursuit of perfection non-negotiable. To my daughter, Meera. I pressed reset when you were born and life has never been the same.

# INDEX

asset management company (AMC), 118

Bombay Stock Exchange (BSE), 102
broad market index, 107, 112, 137

capital appreciation, 97
capital gains tax, 167
cash-flow cell, 166
cash-flow system, 5–8, 14, 19, 70, 73, 166, 190, 208, 215
consumer price index, 101, 103, 105
corporate bond fund, 128

corporate deposits, 84, 94
credit risk funds, 128, 159
cryptocurrency, 210–12

diversification, 123, 132–33, 163, 164

emergency cell, 167–68, 170
emergency fund, 17–21, 23, 70, 74, 117, 158, 167–68, 185, 190, 218, 259
employees' provident fund (EPF), 85, 112, 185
equity funds, 132–33, 138–140, 143, 145, 148, 149, 154, 157, 159, 172–73, 251–52

equity-linked savings
    schemes (ELSSs), 58,
    141–42, 157, 158, 161–62
exchange-traded funds
    (ETFs), 87, 112, 114,
    130–32, 137, 145, 149, 173,
    190, 192, 194, 212
exit costs, 146, 154, 158
exit load, 154, 158–59
expense ratio, 130, 145–47,
    154

Fidelity Investments, 184

Goetting, Marsha A., 203
gold, as an investment
    option, 71, 80, 83, 85–88,
    91–92, 94, 106–111, 117,
    121, 130–32, 144, 149,
    164, 173, 180, 185, 190,
    198–99, 211–12
and real estate, 91, 94, 110,
    173, 211
gold funds, gold bonds, 87,
    94, 121, 130, 132, 173

Home Trade, 119, 209

Income Account, 9–11, 166,
    215
inflation index, 100–01
input price inflation, 106
insurance, 2–3, 9, 17–18, 21,
    26, 29, 30–43. *See also* life
    insurance;
Invest-It Account, 9–14,
    166, 216
Initial Coin Offers (ICOs),
    210

life insurance, 26, 43, 47,
    49–64, 142, 153, 160–63,
    169, 190–91, 196, 204,
    220
bonus, 35, 52–53, 156
endowment insurance
    plan/policy, 51
good time to buy one, 57
how much cover one
    needs, 28, 55,
participating plans, 52,
    156
term cover/term
    insurance plan,
    31, 56, 60, 62, 185,
    222, understanding

products in the market, 50
when one does not need a life cover, 61, which policy to buy and how to buy, 59
lock-in, 142, 157, 158,

'market capitalization', 102
medical cover, medical insurance, 24–27, 29, 31, 38–43, 74, 169, 185, 259
  benefits, 30–31
  critical illness and accident cover, 39
  'family floater', 29
  by office/company, 26
medical emergency, 3, 16, 24, 43
medical insurance policy, 169
  claims, 36
  co-pay clause, 31–32
  disease waiting period, 33
  'pre-existing' disease clause, 32
  price, 50

sub-limits, 34
  'top-up' plan, 38
medium-term bond funds, 128
Mehta, Harshad, 89, 119. *See also* stock market scams
mid-cap index, 105, 112, 137–38
monthly income plans (MIPs), 142
multilevel marketing (MLM) schemes, 119, 209
mutual funds, 21, 25, 55, 58–59, 68, 71, 77, 82, 85, 87, 92, 112, 114, 116, 157, 158, 161, 163, 167, 168, 171–72, 180, 185, 193, 198, 210, 212, 254
  asset management company (AMC), 118
  debt funds, 21–23, 94, 123, 133, 141, 143, 145, 154, 159, 162, 164, 168, 171, 193
  kinds of, 124, 128–30

ultra-short-term fund, 145, 159
direct plan, 145, 146–47
equity funds, 132, 138–140, 145, 148–49, 154, 159, 172, 251, 252
active and passive, 133
balanced funds, 142
index returns, 107, 135
open-ended and closed-end funds, 139
growth, dividend and dividend reinvestment, 140
investment horizon (tenor), 124, 128, 129, 158, 161
liquid funds, 158
how do mutual funds make money, 144,
systematic investment plan (SIP), 147
systematic transfer plan (STP), 148

systematic withdrawal plan (SWP), 141
National Pension Scheme (NPS), 153
net asset value (NAV), 137
Nifty50, 102, 104, 105, 149

real assets, 82–83, 202
real estate, 71, 80, 83–85, 88–94
retirement fund, 47, 172, 192,

Schmall, Vicki L., 187
sector funds, 138, 172
small-cap index, 105, 137
Sovereign Gold Bond Scheme, 132
Spend-It Account, 9–12, 19, 166, 215

third-party agent (TPA), 29

Unit 64 scam, 120
unit-linked insurance plan (ULIP), 45, 55

# ABOUT THE AUTHOR

Monika Halan is a trusted personal-finance writer, speaker and author who helps individuals and families get their money decisions right. Her career spans across media, public policy and financial education. Halan is the founder of Dhan Chakra Financial Education and author of the bestselling book *Let's Talk Money*, which has been translated into Hindi, Marathi, Punjabi and Malayalam; *Let's Talk Mutual Funds*, translated into Hindi and Marathi; and *Let's Talk Legacy*, translated into Hindi. Her podcast *Let's Talk Money with Monika Halan* is available on all major platforms.

She has been, and continues to be, on various committees of the capital-market regulator. She is currently the chairperson of the advisory committee for SEBI's Investor Protection Fund. She has public-policy experience and has served on several high-profile Government of India committees that have changed the regulation around consumer protection in

India: as a member of the task force set up to put in place the Financial Redressal Agency in 2015-16, as a member of the committee on incentives (Bose Committee) in 2015 and as an advisor to the committee on investor awareness and protection (Swarup Committee) in 2009.

On the academic side, Halan has published papers on household finance in some of the top journals in the field. She was a director on the Financial Planning Standards Board of India and is a member of the Editor's Guild. She has worked for publications in India, including *Mint*, *The Economic Times* and *The Indian Express*, and was the editor of *Outlook Money*. She has run four successful TV series around personal finance on NDTV, Zee and Bloomberg India. She holds an MA in economics from the Delhi School of Economics and an MA in journalism studies from the University of Wales. A Yale World Fellow (2011), Halan is based in New Delhi.

Her social media handles are @monikahalan. She can be reached via her site www.monikahalan.com and on mail at mailme@monikahalan.com

## Also by Monika Halan

# HarperCollins *Publishers* India

At HarperCollins India, we believe in telling the best stories and finding the widest readership for our books in every format possible. We started publishing in 1992; a great deal has changed since then, but what has remained constant is the passion with which our authors write their books, the love with which readers receive them, and the sheer joy and excitement that we as publishers feel in being a part of the publishing process.

Over the years, we've had the pleasure of publishing some of the finest writing from the subcontinent and around the world, including several award-winning titles and some of the biggest bestsellers in India's publishing history. But nothing has meant more to us than the fact that millions of people have read the books we published, and that somewhere, a book of ours might have made a difference.

As we look to the future, we go back to that one word—a word which has been a driving force for us all these years.

Read.